MANDALA

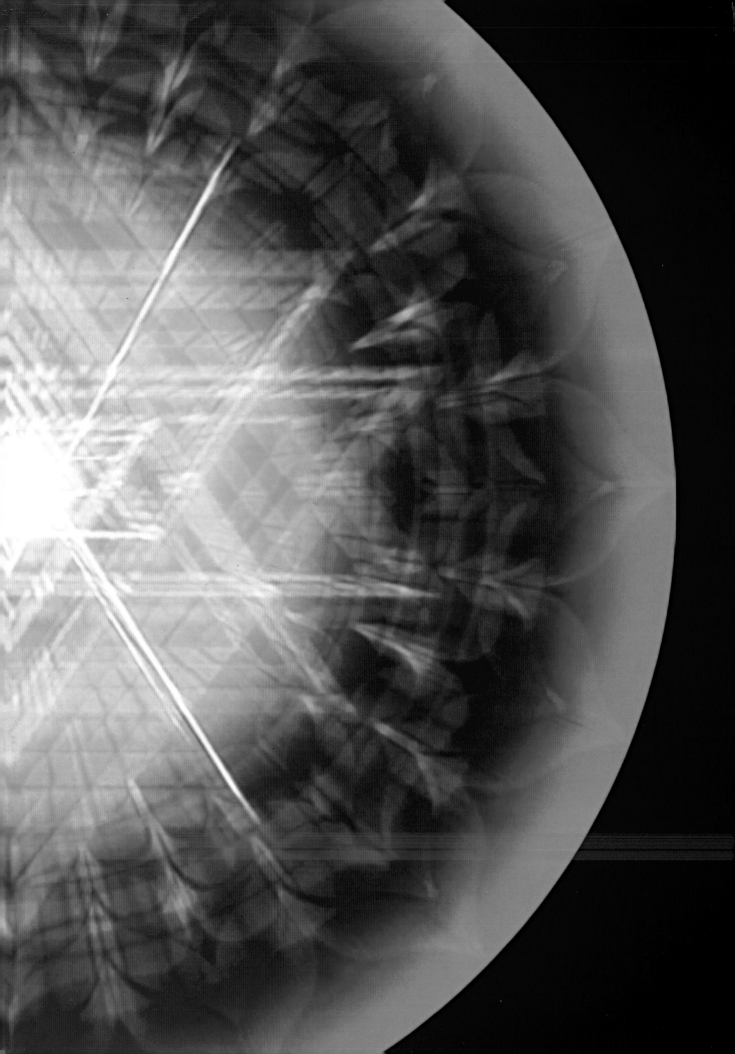

MANDALA

Luminous Symbols for Healing

JUDITH CORNELL

FOREWORD BY

Drs. Joan and Miron Borysenko

This publication was made possible
with the assistance of the Kern Foundation and
the Laurance S. Rockefeller Trust of the Flow Fund

QUEST BOOKS

The Theosophical Publishing House

Wheaton, Illinois, U.S.A.

Quest Books

The Theosophical Publishing House

P.O. Box 270

Wheaton, IL 60189-0270

www.questbooks.net

Library of Congress Cataloging-in-Publication Data

Cornell, Judith

Mandala: luminous symbols for healing / Judith Cornell: foreword by Joan Borysenko

p.   cm.

Includes bibliographical references.

ISBN-13: 978-0-8356-0847-3

ISBN-10: 0-8356-0847-6

1. Self-actualization (Psychology)—Religious aspects.

2. Mandala.   3. Meditation.   4. Holistic medicine.   I. Title.

BV4598.2.C67   1994

291.3'7—dc20   94-18532

CIP

Book and Cover Design by Beth Hansen-Winter

Cover art (*Aum*), title page, and chapter openers by Judith Cornell,

created on a Macintosh 660AV in Adobe Photoshop and Adobe Illustrator

5 4 3 2 * 08 09 10

This book was created on Macintosh computers using Aldus PageMaker, Adobe Photoshop, Adobe Illustrator,
and Aldus FreeHand, is set in Horley Old Style and Felix, and is printed on 128gsm Matt artpaper.

Printed in China

Permission to print the following quoted material is gratefully acknowledged:

From *The Divine Romance* by Paramahansa Yogananda. ©1986. From *Autobiography of a Yogi* by P. Yogananda. ©1946 Paramahansa Yogananda (renewed 1974 Self-Realization Fellowship) ©1981 Self-Realization Fellowship. From *Scientific Healing Affirmations* by P. Yogananda. ©1958, 1962, 1981
(renewed 1986, 1990). From *Man's Eternal Quest and Other Talks* by P. Yogananda. ©1982. From *Self-Realization Magazine*, Vol. 64, Winter 1992.
©1992. From *Where There is Light* by P. Yogananda. ©1988. Reprinted by permission of Self-Realization Fellowship. / From *The Way of the White
Clouds* by Lama Anagarika Govinda. ©Hutchinson & Co. Reprinted by permission of Georges Borchardt, Inc. / From *Introduction to Tantra: A Vision
of Totality* by Lama Yeshe. ©1987 Wisdom Publications. Reprinted by permission of Wisdom Publications, Inc. / From *Tibetan Yoga and Secret Doc-
trines*, Second Edition, edited by W. Y. Evans-Wentz. ©W. Y. Evans-Wentz 1958. Reprinted by permission of Oxford University Press, Inc. / From
Hands of Light by Barbara Ann Brennan. ©1987 by Barbara Ann Brennan. Used by permission of Bantam Books, a division of Bantam Doubleday Dell
Publishing Group, Inc. / From *A Path With Heart* by Jack Kornfield. ©1993 by Jack Kornfield. Used by permission of Bantam Books, a division of
Bantam Doubleday Dell Publishing Group, Inc. / From *Tibetan Buddhist Medicine and Psychiatry* by Terry Clifford. ©1984. Reprinted by permission of
Samuel Weiser, Inc. / From *Sri Chakra* by Sri S. Shankaranarayanan. ©S. Shankaranarayanan. Reprinted by permission of Dipti Publications. / From
The Secret of the Golden Flower, Thomas Cleary, trans. ©1991. Reprinted by permission of HarperCollins Publishers. / From *Mother Earth Spirituality*
by Ed McGaa, Eagle Man. ©1990. Reprinted by permission of HarperCollins Publishers. / From *Answers* by Mother Meera. ©1991 by Mother Meera.
Reprinted by permission of Meeramma Publications, 26 Spruce Lane, Ithaca, NY 14850, Tel. (607)257-1715. / From "The Flowering Earth: Ancient
Wisdom in Mexico," by Mazatl Galindo, *Noetic Sciences Review* (Summer 1993). Reprinted by permission of *Noetic Sciences Review*. / From *Meditations
with Hildegard of Bingen*, edited by Gabriele Uhlein. ©1982. Bear & Co., Inc., P.O. Box 2860 Santa Fe, NM 87504. / From *Hildegard of Bingen's Book of
Divine Works*, edited by Matthew Fox. ©1987, Bear & Co., Inc., P.O. Box 2860, Santa Fe, NM 87504. / From *Unknown Man* by Yatri. ©1988 by Yatri.
Reprinted by permission of Simon & Schuster, Inc. / From *Memories, Dreams, and Reflections*, by C. G. Jung. ©1961, 1962, 1963 and renewed 1989,
1990, 1991 by Random House, Inc. Reprinted by permission of Pantheon Books, a division of Random House, Inc.

To

MARION R. WEBER

gifted visionary of healing arts

CONTENTS

ACKNOWLEDGMENTS

I AM ESPECIALLY INDEBTED TO MARION WEBER FOR HER visionary gifts and support of this project from its inception; to Dr. Willis Harman, president, Winston Franklin, executive director, and Glenn C. Janss, board member, of the Institute of Noetic Sciences, for supporting the healing arts; and to John White and Brenda Rosen at Quest Books, whose enthusiasm made this vision a reality.

I am deeply grateful to those who labored long hours with loving effort to contribute their light to this project: Susan Sopcak for the beautiful instructional color drawings in Chapter 4; Bob Spence and Allen Crider for their helpful support with computer technology; Drs. Joan and Miron Borysenko for their beautiful foreword; Beth Hansen for designing this book as an elegant and inspirational work of art; and Greg and Mary Holden for their careful editing.

I owe heartfelt appreciation to my colleagues and friends for reading and contributing to the book in its various stages: Dr. Michael Flanagin of the C. G. Jung Institute in San Francisco for his scholarship and supportive friendship; Michael and Justine Toms of New Dimensions Radio; Dr. Ulla Sebastian; Nina Menrath; Dr. Bonnie Greenwell; Olga Luchakova, M.D., Ph.D.; Roxanne Lanier; Ann Howell; Lee Sannella, M.D.; Neil Russack, M.D.; Beth Susanne; Anne Herrick; Suzanne Lipsett; and Nancy Grace.

For their support of creative programs for the healing and sacred arts, I would also like to acknowledge Brajesh and the Mount Madonna Community, Ruthann Fowler of the Theosophical Society, the Reverend Dr. Lauren Artress of Grace Cathedral, Tom Valente of Omega Institute, Sr. Christine van Swearingen of the Angela Center, and Patricia Andersson of the Findhorn Foundation.

I also thank those people from my workshops whose beautiful mandalas added inspiration to this book: Bernadette Hotze; Maja Rode; Chryssy Sibbs; Janet Christie-Seely, M.D.; Buffy Hart; Barbara Rifkin; Aida Ferrarone; Jennifer Scott; Susanne Landbauver; Michael Mitchell; Roda Patel, M.D.; Mary Karlton; Joan Malcolm; Pamela Vantress; Jessica Shapley; Myra Herman; H. Margarita Loinaz, M.D.; Sheri Gillette Espar; Christopher Ann Gordon; Jeffry Thomas; Sylvia Nachlinger; Jeanne Jerman Olson; Conny Gerkn; Serin Eggling; Patsy Blackstock; Kay Brockway; and Vanessa Beth Hammack.

The Sacred Circle

When entering the realm of inner vision,

We must create a threefold sacred circle,

Composed of purity, of strength and knowledge

Surrounding us like a protective wall.

The purity of heart creates the lotus-circle;

The adamantine scepters form the second ring:

The power-circle of determined will and higher aims;

The third one is the ring of wisdom-flames.

The threefold magic circle thus unfolded,

Grows with the depth of our heart's vibration,

Grows with the strength of inner penetration,

Grows with the wisdom that knows life and death.

But only when this world becomes a magic circle,

In which each point can be a living centre:

Then we surmount the cause of all illusion,

The riddles of rebirth, of death and dissolution.

Then nothing remains rigid, self-contained;

No point coagulates into a finite 'I,'

Each being in the others is enshrined,

And in the smallest lives infinity.

Then we shall see released to higher norm

This world as essence of the highest mind,

Which, formless though, creates and moves all form,

Inspires and transmutes it, ever unconfined.

    —Lama Anagarika Govinda, *Creative*
      Meditation and Multi-Dimensional
      Consciousness

M IRON AND I WERE THRILLED WHEN JUDITH ASKED US to write this foreword, since both of us have been deeply touched by her synthesis of art, healing, and spirituality. Judith Cornell's work is luminous and glows with an inner light and brilliance. Her gift is in helping us find that luminous core within ourselves—the essential nature that we may know as intuition, creativity, the Higher Self, the Buddha nature, or the Godseed within—so that we may fully express our potential. In the workshops on which this book is based, Judith teaches how to make a place for the sacred in our lives, a temple in which the inner work of healing and transformation can take place. In that temple, as Judith says, we make the invisible visible. We realize the Higher Self and its interconnectedness with all of life. We celebrate transformation and share our gifts with the world.

Our first introduction to art and healing in general and mandalas in particular came at the darkest point of 1978. Winter Solstice marked the beginning of our two-week vacation from Tufts Medical School where we both taught and did medical research. Miron was depressed and out of sorts, virtually incommunicado, leaving me to organize Christmas for our two young sons. Arriving home from a shopping expedition, I was surprised to find Miron revived from his depressed state, having converted our dining room table into what looked like an art studio. Since I had never seen him draw, paint, or express any interest in art at all, I was amazed. Several pieces of white poster board and an assortment of rulers, compasses, protractors, colored pencils, pens, and assorted cans of paint from the garage surrounded him. Flushed and animated, he explained that he had been seized by an inexplicable urge to create something.

And create he did—virtually day and night without stop for the entire two weeks of our vacation. He seemed to be in an altered state in which he needed very little food or rest. The finished product looked like a jewel with many facets, or a temple with many doors. It was filled with spiritual archetypes from both Eastern and Western traditions and had a rich, Byzantine quality to it, as if it had been created by a medieval monk used to illuminating manuscripts. I was awed by its magnificence and its creation, as it were, out of nothing. There were no forms or templates. It had come directly from Miron's unconscious mind. As

I gazed at it, the powerful image seemed to draw me down into my center. When I asked what the image was, Miron replied that he thought such things were called *mandalas,* and what it felt like to him was an outer representation of his inner Self.

In the process of creating the mandala, Miron's depression disappeared. The healing power of the mandala extended not only to him, but to many of the people who took the time to absorb themselves in it. Intrigued, he went off to the bookstore in search of some outer corroboration for his inner process and was just about hit on the head by the proverbial book that falls off the shelf—a book that concerned Carl Jung's personal experiences of mandala drawing and his use of mandala drawing as an agent of healing and transformation for clients who were depressed or in the throes of some other form of crisis. Now there's a synchronicity for you! Having solved his personal "mystery of the healing mandala," Miron went about his usual business of being a medical scientist and educator, and there was a sixteen-year hiatus before he drew another mandala, once again during the Winter Solstice at a time of both inner and outer darkness.

I was writing a book of daily spiritual practices, and Miron had agreed to draw four mandalas—one for each of the seasons. The publisher wanted black-and-white drawings. Fortunately, Miron had taken an afternoon workshop with Judith Cornell one summer, intrigued by her process of "drawing the light from within," and was delighted to work in white on black as you will learn to do in this book. He was just completing the final mandala when Judith phoned to ask us to write this foreword. When he had hung up the phone and come upstairs to tell me, I was writing about Jung's theory of synchronicity, using the example of how Jung had drawn a certain mandala and was puzzled by its distinctly Chinese feel. Shortly thereafter a parcel arrived. It was an ancient Chinese Taoist manuscript on which he was invited to comment.

The synchronicity of Judith calling as Miron was using her technique to create a mandala and as I was reading about Jung's mandala synchronicity was delightful to say the least! It reveals something of the power of the mandala to collapse time and space and bring us into the very heart of healing, the place where you and I dissolve into One. A mandala is like an archetype, a blueprint of some aspect of creation, a hologram. When you create it, or rather tap into it, you enter into the divine consciousness from which that archetype emanated. There is a feeling of "Ah ha!"—of waking up or coming home. A mandala is truly a spiritual experience.

Carl Jung wasn't the first to recognize the healing power of mandalas. The twelfth-century Benedictine nun, Hildegard of Bingen, was a physician, mystic, composer, and artist. She had a series of divine visions, and upon returning to an ordinary state of consciousness, she instructed the nuns of the cloister to draw her visions, many of which were in the form of mandalas. These visions were often accompanied by celestial music, and being a composer, Hildegard was able to capture some of that music, which we can listen to today. In her visions, light and sound were central. Hildegard said, "God was and is without beginning before the creation of the world. God was and is light and radiance and life. And God said, 'Let there be light,' and so were the light and the radiant angels created." When you study Hildegard's mandalas, or listen to her music, you are drawn into the very light of creation itself. You feel inspired, uplifted, and in touch with the Higher Self, what the Buddhists would call "your own true nature."

Judith Cornell is a modern-day Hildegard whose gift is to lead those of us who are willing into a recognition of the light within. Before Hildegard, of course, the Tibetan Buddhists had long used mandalas as part of the spiritual tradition. As we read Judith's description of the way in which the Navajos construct sand mandalas for their healing rituals, then imbue them with spiritual power, we were struck with the parallels to the Tibetan Buddhist Kalachakra Initiation. For the Kalachakra ritual, an incredibly intricate sand mandala is constructed which is said to embody the Kalachakra Deity itself. According to the Dalai Lama, when this mandala is constructed—a formalized procedure that requires teams of five monks working seventeen-hour shifts about four days to complete—something in the atmosphere changes and peace is created. In the 1960s we would have ascribed this change to the "vibes"; now the physicists who study the nature of time, light, and space might have more technical nomenclature. But in some fashion, the mandala creates a harmonic vibration with healing power.

In Judeo-Christian terminology, it is said that the world was created through the word—through sound. Rabbi Lawrence Kushner writes of the Hebrew alphabet, "They are more than just the signs for sounds. They are symbols whose shape and name, placement in the alphabet, and words they begin put each at the center of a unique spiritual constellation. They are themselves holy. They are vessels carrying the light of the Boundless One."

When sound is passed through water, mandalas result! I like to imagine that each one of our cells vibrates with the mandalas of its DNA. In fact, in *Meaning and Medicine*, Dr. Larry Dossey cites the work of a Japanese geneticist, Dr. Susomo Ohno. Dr. Ohno assigned a musical note to each of the four nucleotides that make up DNA. With the help of his wife Midori, a musician, they made a score of the DNA from several species and made recordings of the music performed by concert musicians. These DNA compositions are said to be supremely inspiring and melodic, moving the listeners to tears! They are like sound mandalas—indeed alive in a special sense.

When music really touches us, we feel "thrilled" by it, as if it has truly entered our bodies. And indeed it does. It resonates with the music that is already being produced within us. Judith suggests that you do the magnificent meditations in this book along with inspiring music. The combination of the sound, your intention, and the words that Judith has written can bring you into one of the cosmic mandalas, harmonizing your body in the way that the Kalachakra mandala harmonizes the energy of a city. Her meditations, which are based on years of practice and a deep and intimate understanding of mantra, yantra, light, and spirit, truly open the door to transformation. The mandala drawings that you will bring forth after these meditations may astonish you, and they surely have the power to transform you.

As I prepared to write this foreword, I was feeling depressed, like Miron was in 1978. So I began with Judith's meditation on asking for a personal healing symbol. What came to me was a cup and saucer. Fortunately, I trusted in her admonition not to throw out your images if they seem prosaic or disappointing. As I stayed with the cup and saucer, a six-pointed star formed in the bottom of the cup. This Star of David is also the symbol of the fourth chakra—the heart chakra—and represents the union of the masculine and feminine principles. I drew the cup and saucer as seen from above—a circle within a circle—with the star inside. As I embellished the image, a hexagonal symmetry formed, and I ended up with a mandala of six angels representing love, will, care, song, pray, and play. I felt a healing in bringing forth the mandala, and I feel a continued healing in looking at it as it rests against my Stylewriter printer!

Nature, of course, is the most fertile source of mandalas. Most flowers are mandalas, and what more sacred circles could you find than sun and moon? A study in the journal *Science* indicates that post-surgical patients whose rooms viewed nature healed sooner and left the hospital faster than those whose rooms faced a brick wall. Many hospitals have recognized the importance of creating a healing environment that utilizes light, sound, color, images, and nature to maximize the body's own healing potential. A hospital in Bend, Oregon is designed so that rooms face either east or west, according every patient a view of either a sunrise or a sunset. A hospital in Shreveport, Louisiana has a horticultural therapy room. It would be fascinating to study the healing potential of mandala drawing in a hospital setting.

Whether mandalas come into being as part of our individual healing process, or whether they have been handed down through the centuries as a healing for us all, each has a uniquely transformative energy which lives on in the person who creates or is touched by it. Even if the mandala is destroyed (as in the Navajo and Tibetan sand mandala traditions), what is destroyed in physical form remains in subtle form, and if we have been touched by it, it lives on in the very structure of our cells and psyches. Miron and I are confident that you will be transformed by your participation in Judith's book, as those who have taken part in her workshops have been. And we are also confident that your transformation will, in turn, be a part of the healing of our world.

Each of us is part of the great mandala of creation, a mandala in the making, a mandala that we can shape with our love and live with a smile.

Joan Borysenko
April, 1994

INTRODUCTION

In the act of healing, symbols work upon the patient who is vulnerable, open, and ready to experience them. He identifies with them in the form of the sacred images . . . They transform him and allow him to partake of their hidden power.

—Donald Sandner, *Navaho Symbols of Healing*

Merging Art, Science, and Ancient Wisdom

THIS BOOK IS A CONVERGENCE OF EASTERN AND Western thought—merging the meditative practice of sacred art, the insights of quantum physics into the nature of light, and the ancient wisdom. Each chapter is a blend of spiritual philosophy, transpersonal psychology, and exercises designed to promote healing of mind, body, and soul. This approach results from a time many years ago when I created mandalas when I had cancer and experienced a spiritual awakening. This creative process helped me to integrate the reductionism of the scientific worldview with my intuitive experiences of wholeness and luminous states of consciousness. The sacred symbol of the mandala enabled me

FIG. 0.1. This mandala drawing by Janet Christie-Seely, M.D., had a great transformative effect on her. She says:

The mandala is a magnifying glass or mirror—for all of us. The scene below is Glencoe, my favorite glen in the Scottish highlands and the birthplace of my grandfather, a Gaelic-speaking, Presbyterian, medical missionary in China. I, too, am a missionary for the new age in the medical world. The workshop helped me epitomize my own transformation.

Why Create a Mandala?

♦ Because it has the regenerative and curative power to activate the latent powers of the mind. The meditative process helps to focus and open the heart to the healing power of unconditional love.

♦ Because it has a calming and relaxing effect on the mind and body, thus focusing and strengthening the will to heal.

♦ Because it can bring joy as it facilitates the healing of a sense of psychological fragmentation.

♦ Because it can make the invisible visible—expressing paradoxical situations or patterns of ultimate reality that can be expressed in no other way.

♦ Because it can reveal unity between human existence and the structure of the cosmos—opening up a perspective in which things can be understood as a whole.

♦ Because it can give form and expression to an intuitive insight into spiritual truth by releasing the inner light of the soul.

Modern research methods have demonstrated the power of the mind to influence the outcome of medical treatments—provided that the patient believes in them—suggesting that untapped mental power exists for healing all types of physical and mental maladies. Release of this power by developing such self-healing skills as meditation, visualization, and positive thinking—combined with relaxation, physical exercise, and improved nutrition—can do much to improve the general level of health.[1]

—Steven F. Brena, M.D.

not only to find the healing power within myself but also to recover from a sense of psychological fragmentation. During the healing process, I came to experience and express mystical states of consciousness that, until then, had remained outside my grasp. Since that time I have taught the process of mandala making in workshops to hundreds of people, all of whom have created mandalas to facilitate their own physical or psychological healing and spiritual transformation.

The deeper revelations of this book are based on spiritual intuition gained from my personal practice of Raja Yoga, the "royal" or highest path in Hindu philosophy leading to union of soul with spirit through meditation, and from my study of the Eastern traditions of the yoga of sacred art. The ultimate aim of these practices is Self-realization—the recovery of one's authentic Self, *not* the ego-personality bound by one's individual circumstances. This greater Self is an aspect of transcendental Reality. The recovery of this Self, synonymous with enlightenment, is the mystical experiential knowing and remembering in mind, body, and soul that we are one with God.

A *mandala*, the Sanskrit word for "circle," is a concrete symbol of its creator's absorption into a sacred center. In its most elevated form, the sacred circle mirrors an illumined state of consciousness through a symbolic pattern—making the invisible visible. It is meant to draw both creator and viewer into an encounter with animating sources of numinous energy. The Navajo call this center "a spiritual place of emergence" for sacred imagery. By focusing on it, both mandala artist and meditator can open to the divine energies of deities and to the contents of his or her own spiritual and psychological self. When a practitioner willfully illuminates and embodies a sacred image from within the psyche while in a meditative state, spiritual transformation, physical healing, and the integration of personality fragments can result.

In spiritual traditions worldwide, mandalas focus and reflect the spiritual content of the psyche for both maker and viewer. They are used as a healing and transforming art in Native American sand painting, Hindu and Tibetan Buddhist rituals, and modern psychotherapy. In Jungian psychology, the mandala brings about healing in a type of psychological event called a crisis of transition. Here the ego fragments and is in danger of collapsing; the mandala forges a new relationship of the ego to the Self. Art therapists and psychologists routinely observe that the circle plays a healing role in patients with life-threatening diseases.

The illustrations in this book include both mandalas drawn from recognized spiritual traditions and mandalas produced by participants in my workshops, most of whom are neither trained healers nor experienced artists. Mandalas from every source share an arresting beauty and universal appeal.

The Mandala and Holistic Medicine

Despite the great advances in modern medicine, there is growing discontent with the restrictive view of Western medical science and practice that focuses exclusively on the biochemical operation of the body, disregarding the human mind and spirit. A growing number of physicians have begun to incorporate holistic techniques such as the art of the mandala, yoga, creative visualization, and meditation into their practice. One such physician is Dr. Janet Christie-Seely, associate professor at the Department of Family Medicine at the University of Ottawa in Canada. During one of my workshops in Scotland, Dr. Seely used the mandala to gain intuitive insights into her professional and personal role in advancing the practice of medicine (see Fig. 0.1). She described her experience as follows:

With the power of your mind you can work changes in the life in the body as well as in the body itself. . . . Mind [consciousness or soul, including intelligence, will, and feeling] can enable you to do anything you want, but you must experiment first in little things until you fully develop that power. If you don't constantly work at developing mind power, don't try suddenly to depend wholly on it. . . . those who are fanatical and refuse medical help when they need it often do great injury to themselves. . . . You must use common sense.[2]

—Paramahansa Yogananda

In the meditation I asked for an image to represent standing on my own two feet—personally and professionally—and to my surprise what came to me was a soaring seagull, with its head turned. So I figured that flying was even better than standing. Around the gull is blue sky and the sun shedding new light on the cloudy landscape of the old: personal joy, high self-esteem, and freedom, and professionally, a new way of looking at illness that I have helped bring about, compared to the linear, reductionist, limited view of disease and causality of the old medicine. The gull's head is turning in the new direction compared to the phoenix of the Aesculapian (medical) symbol with its snake and staff. But the gull stays within the symbol (medicine needs to be transformed from within).

Dr. Seely's insight points the way to an exciting new technology of healing, one which brings together body, mind, and spirit and focuses on the whole person.

FIG. 0.2. *Atomistic Paradox,* 1980, OIL PAINTING BY AUTHOR.

This painting arose during meditation as a result of my asking the following question: "What is the underlying essence of all reality?"

"Light," answered an intuitive voice.

This response triggered a spontaneous spiritual awakening to the nature of our human evolution that greatly altered my own consciousness. I saw luminous human bodies without form—a transparency of light which some have called the astral or energy body. Each stage of human evolution flashed before me as an upward spiral of spiritual development into divine realization. I saw human beings transformed into more and more refined and transparent bodies of light, gifted with the divine power to structure atomic energies into any form imaginable. This quantum leap in consciousness transformed my understanding of art as a separate discipline to one that was integrally connected with science and ancient wisdom.

After completing this painting, I came to a greater intuitive understanding of the nature of atomic energies which consciousness creatively directs and continually restructures into diverse molecular configurations.

Creating Mandalas to Facilitate Healing

Mandalas can be used to supplement and enhance Western medicine. An example is the story of a young woman I'll call Sally. Sally came to me for help in using art as a way to heal. Several days before, she had been diagnosed with thyroid cancer. Surgery was to take place in ten days. She had great fear and told me that she felt like curling up into a fetal position and doing nothing.

Over the next eight days, I instructed Sally to make three mandalas. She used the meditation and drawing techniques described in Chapters 1, 2, 3, and 4 for creating and illuminating personal healing symbols. After drawing this series, Sally sharply focused her life force and strengthened her will to live. She also became more centered, peaceful, and grounded, and was able to call on her friends and loved ones for the psychological support she needed to cope with her medical ordeal.

When she entered the hospital for surgery, Sally placed her three mandalas on the wall above her bed so she could focus on these life-affirming images. Three weeks later, Sally wrote a radiant letter to say that the doctors who had removed the tumor had done many lab tests and could only find a few cancer cells left. They were perplexed by this, but told her she did not need any more surgery or treatment.

If Sally had used the mandala in the traditional way of the Navajo,

she would first go through a purification ritual prescribed by a healer. Navajo ritual healing is based on their cultural beliefs and spiritual mythologies. Purification rituals may take the form of a sweat lodge ceremony for healing, dressing in special clothes, and abstaining from certain kinds of work or foods. A participant in a Navajo healing ritual does not construct the mandala herself; this is done by those specially trained in constructing healing symbols. These artisans chant special healing songs while carefully constructing a sand painting large enough for the patient to sit on.

After the mandala is completed, food is brought for the workers. The medicine man then blesses the mandala with pollen and a caller announces the healing ceremony. The healer then guides the patient to sit in the middle of the painting facing east. The patient is expected to fully participate in the healing by absorbing psychologically and spiritually the energies of these sacred healing symbols.

In the final stages of the ritual, the medicine man evokes the deities and acts as a channel for their divine energies. He directs this numinous spiritual energy into the mandala and into the patient by touching the heads of the sand figures and the patient's head, neck, chest, arms, and legs—all the while chanting special sounds. Finally, there are rituals of release for the patient, the healer, and the audience from the powers invoked. Then the sand mandala is destroyed.

Hiranya, 1981, oil painting by author

Fig. 0.3 (right). *E=mc²*, oil painting by author.

I made this mandala painting in 1979. As I worked on it, I came to believe that the painting had something to do with light and physics. To understand its meaning, I began to research scientific literature. One day, while reading about Albert Einstein's famous equation *E=mc²* (energy = mass times the speed of light squared), I realized that this painting represented a visual symbol of his equation. Through the painting, I understood the dual nature of light—its *particle* aspect and its *wave* aspect. At a deeper level, I comprehended the divine intelligence that creates an infinite variety of forms from light, and I perceived that humankind is beginning to participate more fully in this act of creation.

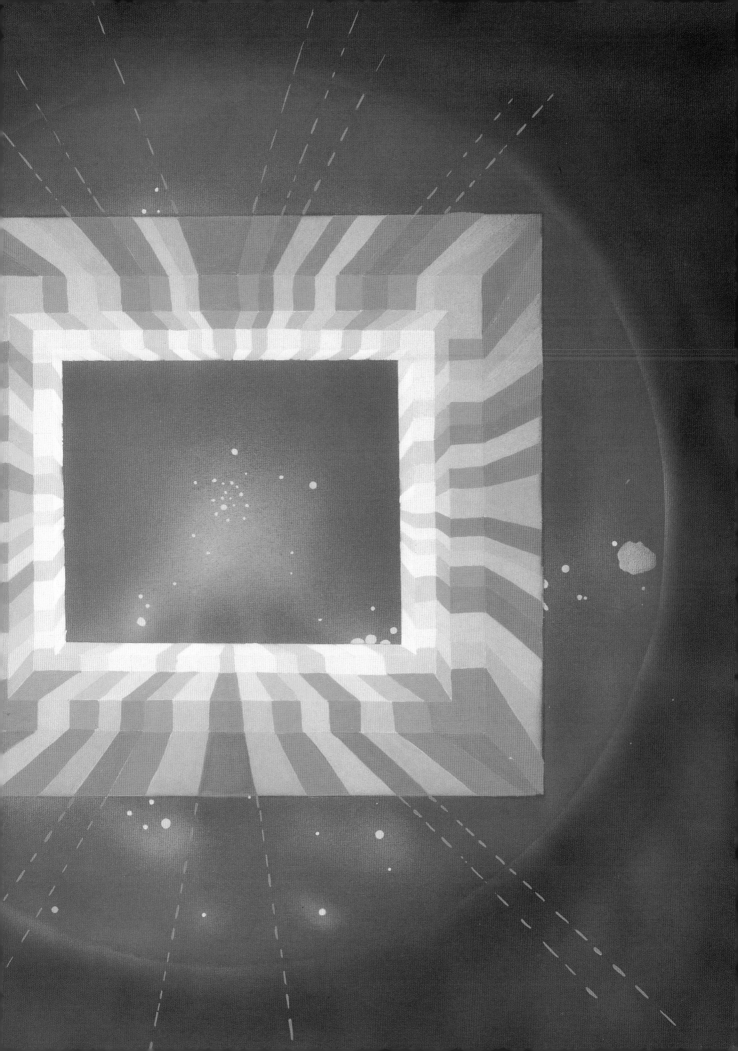

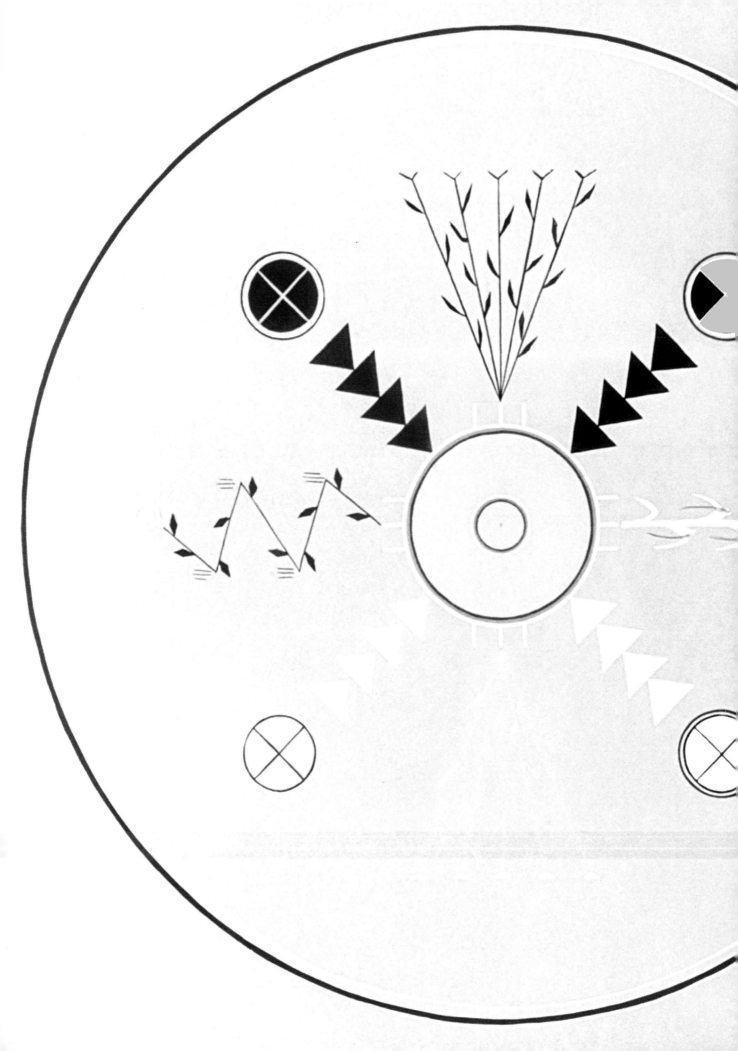

Summary

Modern science does not yet understand the relationship between the body and the mind. But it is not necessary to wait for science to catch up to benefit from creating mandalas. Neither Sally's nor Dr. Seely's story is objective proof that drawing mandalas can cure cancer or facilitate transformative insights, and I am not citing them as scientific examples. It is also not necessary to have a religious belief or make a permanent commitment to one point of view. The best way to proceed with the exercises in this book is to temporarily suspend any disbelief you might have, and rest your faith on this healing possibility. Keep an open mind and experiment with this process yourself.

Notes

[1] Steven F. Brena, M.D., "The Placebo Effect: Is Modern Medicine Discovering the Power of the Mind?" *Self-Realization* 63 (Fall 1992): 54.

[2] Paramahansa Yogananda, *The Divine Romance* (Los Angeles: Self-Realization Fellowship, 1986), 164–65.

Fig. 0.4. *Emergence Place.* Navajo Sandpainting. Reproduced by permission of the Wheelwright Museum of the American Indian, Santa Fe, No. P1-16.

CHAPTER 1:

MANDALAS AS PATTERNS OF LIGHT AND SOUND

What we call the 'dark background of consciousness' is understood to be a higher consciousness; thus our concept of the 'collective unconscious' would be the European equivalent of buddhi—*the enlightened mind.*

—C. G. Jung, foreword to The Tibetan Book of the Great Liberation

It is the role of religious symbols to give a meaning to the life of man . . . Modern man does not understand how much his 'rationalism' (which has destroyed his capacity to respond to numinous symbols and ideas) has put him at the mercy of the psychic 'underworld'. . . We have stripped all things of their mystery and numinosity; nothing is holy any longer.

—C. G. Jung, Man and His Symbols

Only he who, while fully recognizing and understanding his Western heritage, penetrates and absorbs the heritage of the East, can gain the highest values of both worlds and do justice to them. East and West are the two halves of our human consciousness, comparable to the two poles of a magnet, which condition and correspond to each other and cannot be separated. Only if man realizes this fact will he become a complete human being.

—Lama Anagarika Govinda, *Creative Meditation and Multi-Dimensional Consciousness*

FROM A HINDU PERSPECTIVE THE UNIVERSE IS SAID TO have evolved from pure Consciousness through the sacred sound of *Aum (Om)*. This sacred *Aum* vibration emitted and divided itself into infinite patterns of conscious light and sound frequencies. Consciousness evolved in a downward spiral, proceeding from subtle frequencies to the most dense patterns of light and sound, which culminated in the creation of the physical world—the stars, the planets, and all life forms on Earth, of which humankind is a part.

Sacred Circle of Highest Bliss

The mandala in its highest tantric representation is a symbolic pattern of light and sound, reflecting the evolution of the universe and the supreme, blissful realization of the soul or higher-Self within the human body/mind—remembering and experiencing itself as a spark of the original pure clear light of consciousness. Lama Anagarika Govinda describes his discovery in a Tibetan temple ruins of the great mandala:

With a strange feeling of expectancy I entered into the death-like stillness of a half-dark room, in which the secrets of centuries seemed to be present and to weigh upon me like the fate of an unfulfilled past . . .

FIG 1.1. VIBRANT PATTERNS OF CONSCIOUSNESS.

These mandalas represent the core structure of a Tibetan mandala. The small circle in the center of the mandala represents pure mind or clear light. This "true state" of the mind is called the clear light of consciousness.

The computer-generated mandala above is intended to give you an intuitive sense of illumined consciousness as a sacred vibrating pattern of light and sound. A central doctrine of Tantra is that every thought or idea originates in sound and is manifested as patterns of light, giving to the phenomenal world a sense of solid form.

I stood in the Holy of Holies of a mystery temple, the chamber of initiation, in which the great mandala, *'the Sacred Circle of Highest Bliss,' is revealed before the eyes of the initiate, in all its manifold forms of celestial splendor, divine figures and cosmic symbols . . . For almost a year it formed the centre of my religious life—and even then I realized that I had only lifted a tiny corner of the veil that hides the supreme realization of this profoundest of all profound Tantras . . .*

It contains the complete process of a world creation from the deepest centre of consciousness—the unfoldment of forms from the formless state of undifferentiated emptiness and unlimited potentiality—through the germ-syllables of the subtle elementary principles and the crystal-lisation of their essential forms and colours into a concentric image of the universe, spread out in ever widening rings of materialising worlds. Their essential and timeless centre is represented by the symbol of Mount Meru, the stable axis and the ideal cross-section of the universe, in which the hierarchy of divine beings and realms of existence—the increasingly intensified and purified manifestations, or higher dimen-sions of consciousness—*are present.*[1]

FIG. 1.2. *Mandala of Manjushri Thangka,* 17TH-18TH CENTURY. COURTESY OF THE ASIAN ART MUSEUM OF SAN FRANCISCO, THE AVERY BRUNDAGE COLLECTION, B63 D6.

Tibetan mandalas are visual representations of Buddhist scripture, created in a state of prayer and devotional chanting. Tibetan monks train many years to learn the scriptural meanings and precise ways of drawing the images. There is no creative invention along the way. Lama Yeshe says:

Tantra provides powerful methods for getting in touch with our essential whole-ness. Tantric art is filled with potent symbols of the unity and completeness characteristic of our fully realized potential. The image of male and female deities in sexual embrace—taken by some early Western interpreters of Tibetan Bud-dhism as a sign of its degeneration—is a symbolic portrayal of the inner unifica-tion of our own male and female energies . . . their embrace symbolizes the aim of the very highest tantric practices: generation of a most subtle and blissful state of mind that, by its very nature, is supremely suited to penetrate ultimate reality and free us from all delusion and suffering.[2]

Materials

◆ Scissors

◆ Pencil sharpener

◆ Records or tapes of inspirational music

◆ Audio tapes of the guided meditations in this book (these can be obtained by contacting Quest Books at 1-800-669-9425).

American Art Supplies

◆ 3 sheets 19" x 25" black Strathmore Charcoal paper or black Canson Ingres Vidalon, Canson Mitentes black charcoal drawing paper or large pads (approximately 16 sheets of paper per pad), or a large sheet of Arches black cover stock.

◆ 2 white Berol Prismacolor pencils

The paper amounts listed here should be enough to complete the exercises in the first four chapters.

European Art Supplies

◆ 3 large sheets 700 mm x 500 mm black Daler Ingres Rowney charcoal paper (made in England), or black Canson Ingres Vidalon 50 x 65 cm, or Canson Mitentes drawing paper (made in Annonay, France). There are other black pastel papers in Europe. You may need to experiment with them to see which side of the paper is best to draw on for creating the most radiant scale of light.

◆ 2 white Berol Karisma Colour pencils (made in England)

H. Margarita Loinaz, M.D.

Lama Govinda experienced the mandala through the lens of Tibetan Buddhist culture. But no matter what cultural lens is used, the symbol of a circle which contains the whole world and the various evolutionary levels of consciousness is powerful and universal.

Unlike those who created the Tibetan temple of the great mandala, most of us are not in an illumined state of consciousness. Because of this, and because we identify ourselves with the physical body/mind, we experience much suffering due to the ignorance of our actions which do not admit to our divinity and ultimate relationship with divine consciousness. But deep within our psyches, this universal light of consciousness awaits our remembering and expressing who we really are. This chapter lays the groundwork you need to create a healing mandala by gaining access to the soul-light within you, to express creatively the essential beauty and wholeness of your true nature.

Anne Gerow

Author

FIG. 1.3. CREATING A SCALE
OF LIGHT.

A Symbolic Healing

We begin to prepare for a symbolic healing by first learning (in Exercise 1) to work with black drawing paper and white drawing pencil to create a sense of light emanating from the paper. This will be followed by a guided meditation to inspire you for Exercise 2, in which you will again use black paper and white pencil to create an expanding pattern of light—a drawing reflecting your unique pattern of inner light.

Exercise 1: *Creating a Scale of Light*

In this exercise you will create the scale of light (see Fig. 1.3), a basic tool for perceiving your consciousness as a pattern of light while working with black-and-white materials. The following are suggestions for preparing the paper.

1. Fold one large sheet of drawing paper in half, as in Fig. 1.4.

2. Cut the paper on the fold and set aside the extra piece.

3. Fold the half-sheet of paper so that the largest section is a square.

4. Cut off the smaller rectangle section. Use this rectangle for practicing the drawing technique in this exercise. Save the square paper that is left for use in Exercise 2.

5. With your smaller rectangle of black paper and two sharpened white pencils in front of you visualize the following:

   ◆ Imagine that when you put a white pencil stroke down on the black paper you will bring your creative spirit into the precreative darkness.

   ◆ Visualize the energy of the white pencil being infused and directed by the inner light of your consciousness.

   ◆ Envision the black paper to be the womb of Mother Earth—absorbing and reflecting your light to give birth to new forms.

   ◆ Think and visualize light as you draw. Your drawing will be a physical expression and reflection of your inner light of spirit.

6. Beginning anywhere on the black paper, use your white drawing pencil to create a scale of light. It is important to keep your pencil sharp in order to achieve a smooth transition from white to black. Hold your pencil at an angle close to the paper in a way that allows you to move your arm and wrist freely.

7. Start at the light end of the scale by making heavy, smooth strokes. Lighten the pressure of the pencil as you proceed to the darkest end of the scale, making the white of the pencil gradually fade into the black paper.

8. The scale should show a smooth transition from pure white light through a gradual fading of light and on into blackness. You may have to go over the scale a few times to smooth out the transition from white to black.

9. Try out different ways of making a scale of light. The scale can be thick, thin, wide, long, curved, square, and so on. Remember that your pencil and paper are pure energy and that you are actually drawing light and energy. When you feel that you have learned to make a simple scale of light with smooth transitions, proceed to the meditation and second exercise.

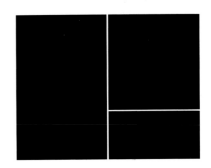

FIG. 1.4. PAPER PREPARATION.

Fold the paper in half as indicated by the vertical white line. You will need only half a sheet for the exercises in this chapter. Save the other half for the color exercises in Chapter 4.

For the first practice exercise, *Creating a Scale of Light*, use the smaller rectangle to draw on.

MEDITATION: *Remembering Who You Are*

Once you have done this meditation and reflected on the experience, you will be ready, in the second part of the drawing exercise, to produce your unique pattern of light and consciousness. Before you begin, sharpen your white pencils. Then place the square sheet of paper and your pencils next to you.

Sit in an upright position in a chair, with your back straight, feet flat on the floor, and hands comfortably in your lap. If you wish, play soft inspirational or sacred music in the background.

❖

Slowly take three deep breaths. On each exhalation, release all tension or negative thoughts from your mind and body.

❖

Keeping your heart open and receptive, close your eyes. Imagine a ball of rainbow-colored light at the top of your head. Visualize it descending into the center of your brain.

❖

Concentrate on that glowing energy, and direct it down through your neck and into your heart, feeling warmth and love. Continue directing it downward into your stomach and the rest of your organs and finally down through your legs to the soles of your feet and into the ground.

❖

Now visualize this healing and centering energy and light coming back up from the ground and up the back of your legs. Slowly direct it up through the core of your spine and back into your head.

❖

Imagine yourself being lifted gently into the universe. Keeping a sense of your meditative posture, see and feel yourself floating gently in outer space, surrounded by the stars and planets.

❖

Realize that your body and the manifest universe are an inseparable cosmic creation of vibrating atomic polarities.

❖

Realize that all the atoms in your physical body are billions of years old—composed from the exploding light of ancient stars and other electromagnetic energies.

❖

Imagine yourself being pulled into a black hole of radiation, going past time and space into the dark womb of the universe. The silence of this black hole is beyond description—it is intelligence, as yet unthinking. Experience the peace and bliss of this all-pervasive intelligence.

❖

Imagine this intelligence beginning to think and creatively to dream. Suddenly you experience a roaring sound and a spark of visible light spreads. Somehow originating in the sound, the light begins to radiate throughout the darkness. Creation has begun. You perceive vast clouds of many-colored lights that are the formation of galaxies and all the other creations of Earth, including your physical body.

❖

Imagine yourself as the soul within the human body and that the sun's rainbow-colored light is *entering* into your physical body. Now imagine streams of electromagnetic energy and waves of visible light pouring *out* of your body and creatively interweaving with the streams of energy that compose the universe.

❖

Meditate for a moment on this web of light streams that connects your soul, mind, and physical body to the universe. Realize that through the divine inner light of your consciousness you are participating in the creation of this tapestry of light and life.

❖

Gently bring your focus back to the planet Earth and the spot you occupy physically. See with new eyes the white pencil and black paper that is in front of you. Visualize the paper and pencil as atoms of pulsating energy. Holding this perception in your mind's eye, proceed with the next drawing exercise.

❖

Light is the first begotten, and the first emanation of the Supreme, and Light is Life, says the Evangelist and the Kabalist. Both are electricity—the life principle . . . pervading the universe, the electric vivifier of all things . . . From its swelling electric bosom spring matter and spirit. Within its beams lie the beginnings of all physical and chemical action, and of all cosmic and spiritual phenomena; it vitalizes and disorganizes; it gives life and produces death, and from its primordial point gradually emerged into existence the myriads of worlds . . .[3]

—H. P. Blavatsky

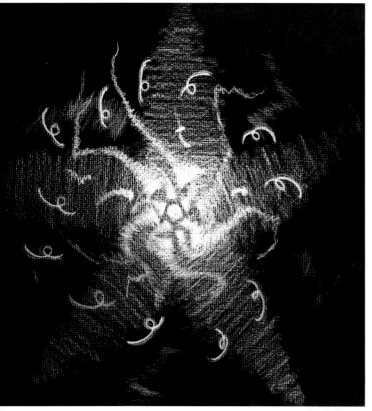

Pamela Vantress

Susan Sopcak

Jennifer Scott

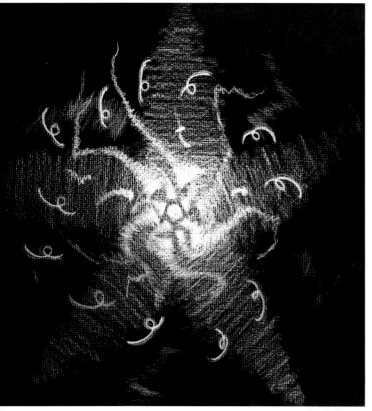

Susanne Landbauver

Exercise 2: *Expanding the Light Within*

This exercise will help you spiral inward, open your heart to unconditional love, and release fear. Breaking through that inner barrier to reality will enable you to experience the balance, wholeness, and spiritual light within yourself. In this exercise, you will create a vibrant pattern of energy by using repetitive scales of light imaginatively. Doing this exercise will help release fear of the drawing process so that you may begin expressing your inner light of consciousness in a way that is joyful, radiant, and alive. The examples in this chapter illustrate the many ways people have spontaneously reflected their intuitive state of consciousness just by repeating the scale of light.

1. Take out your square sheet of paper and your white pencils. It is easier to get a beautiful scale of light with the white pencils if they are kept sharp at all times.

2. Using the white pencil, place a dot in the center of the black paper. This dot, called a Bindu in tantric art, is a symbol of Supreme Consciousness. It represents the sacred center, mirroring the spiritual center within you—the midpoint between your eyebrows. This place between the brows is called the third or spiritual eye.

3. Before beginning, center yourself in a meditative state. Focus on your third eye and keep your heart open and loving. Play some sacred music that uplifts your consciousness to a sense of the Divine.

4. Start at the center of the paper, where you placed your dot, and begin drawing the scale of light. Work from the center of the paper outward, like an unfolding galaxy, repeating the scale of light and changing its size and shape in response to your intuitive insights gained from the meditation. Focus intently on creating a sense of illumination as you work. Think of your light spiraling outward as part of a galactic dance. You can turn the paper as you work.

5. Repeat the scale, change the size and direction, overlap the scales of light, and continue this meditation until you have expanded from the center point. Let your intuition guide you and be open to the flow of Divine love through your hands, into the pencil, and onto the paper.

6. Each time you feel fearful or stuck, breathe gently and focus on keeping your heart open. Have the courage to explore your unique pattern and expression of spiritual light.

7. When you are finished, hang up the image that has emerged and look at it. Let it speak to you in the silence of your heart.

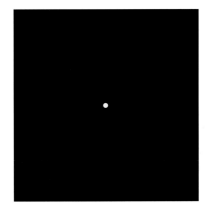

FIG. 1.5.

Express your unique pattern of light, using the meditation as an inspiration. Begin by placing a white dot in the middle of the square, working from the center outward, like an unfolding galaxy.

Mary Karlton

What Has Happened? What Have You Done?

According to Yogananda and all great masters, humankind's greatest goal is to overcome the cosmic illusion that all forms are separate and distinct: to rise above the laws of polarities that give us day and night, death and life, good and evil, pleasure and pain, light and shadow, and to experience ourselves and the universe as the totality of God's Absolute Nature—the One, illumined throughout by cosmic light.[4] The pattern you created from the scales of light reflects a unique part of the totality of this pervasive cosmic light. It is an expression of integration—and integration is the essence of healing at the most fundamental level.

The preceding meditation and exercise function as a ritual to integrate the Eastern view that we have evolved from a pattern of consciousness, light, and sound with the Western perspective that material reality is in essence energy. The purpose of this ritual was to help you remember the descent of the soul into physical light and duality—your forgotten memory of the origin of the universe and your own evolution within it. By identifying with the forces of creation and entering into them symbolically, you have begun to access the power to re-create the world as one. This means that you have begun to experience a state of health—which is simply wholeness.

Physics, Art, and the Science of Consciousness

In recent times there has been a proliferation of literature drawing parallels between holonomic theories of light, quantum physics, and the mystics' view of integral wholeness.[6] As a culture we have looked primarily to Western science to alleviate human suffering and to understand our purpose in the scheme of things. But is science capable of freeing us from all suffering? Can science guide us to a direct mystical experience of our divinity through the bliss of integrating with the One Light? Is there a parallel between modern physics and the yoga of sacred art regarding the nature of light and consciousness?

Enlightenment and release from suffering are the point of the traditional practice of yoga mirrored in tantric art. As a spiritual and practical psychology it encompasses knowledge of the electromagnetic field studied by physicists because it is *inclusive* of all levels of consciousness and "light" from gross to subtle. In the East, tantra and other forms of yoga are considered subjective sciences. In the Hindu and Buddhist traditions, the practice of art is a creative process of alchemy that integrates spiritual consciousness with the gross aspect of the physical body and art materials (e.g., divine love flowing from

As steps in man's awakening, the Lord inspires scientists to discover, at the right time and place, the secrets of His creation. Many modern discoveries help man to apprehend the cosmos as a varied expression of one power—light, guided by divine intelligence.[5]

—Paramahansa Yogananda

your hands into the paper and pencils). The ultimate aim of these
practices is enlightenment, or total healing—physical, mental, and
spiritual transformation and blissful integration of the Self with the
One Light.

Physics, on the other hand, cannot encompass the subtle light and
mystical realms of consciousness or sacred art because it is *exclusive*. In
the process of studying light and fragmenting the atom into its various
parts, physics *excluded* the human attributes of emotion, intuition, creativity, soul, and consciousness. The Western scientific worldview based
on reductionist experiments has evolved over hundreds of years. During
that time, scientific investigators performing countless experiments have
"discovered" and "proven" that physical light is dual in nature, expressed either as a wave or as a particle of matter. As Ken Wilber points
out in "Physics, Mysticism and the New Holographic Paradigm," this
approach of physics to the study of matter and energy is considered
from the perspective of the perennial philosophy to be the most frag-
mented and to be on the lowest realm of the hierarchy of consciousness:

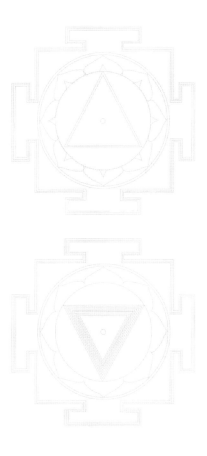

> . . . *for example the study of biology uses physics, but the study of*
> *physics does not use biology . . . The higher [realm of consciousness]*
> *transcends but includes the lower—not vice versa . . .*

> *In short, speaking of these subatomic particles and waves and fields,*
> *the physicist says, "They all interpenetrate one another and exist*
> *together." Now a less than cautious person, seeing that the mystic and*
> *the physicist have used precisely the same words to talk about their*
> *realities, would thereby conclude that the realities must also be the*
> *same. And they are not.*[7]

The mechanistic parameters of Western science have permeated
our perceptions, our thinking, our emotions, and even our ways of
relating to one another. The result has been nothing less than a total
fragmentation of our collective consciousness. The scientific worldview
has led to the neglect of our intuitive spiritual perceptions and the
creative development of our souls—which, according to the sages of the
East, are there to lead to greater understanding and release us from
ignorance, laws of duality, and suffering. Because it is constrained
within the laws of polarities, science by itself cannot help us to achieve
wholeness. As Yogananda says:

> *The entire phenomenal world is under the inexorable sway of polarity;*
> *no law of physics, chemistry, or any other science is ever found free from*
> *inherent opposite or contrasted principles.*

Patricia Andersson

Physical science, then, cannot formulate laws outside of maya*: the very fabric and structure of creation. . . . Future scientists can do no more than probe one aspect after another of her varied infinitude. Science thus remains in a perpetual flux, unable to reach finality . . .*[8]

A Scientific Revolution

In 1873, physicist James Clerk Maxwell launched a revolution in the scientific worldview. He was able to bring Michael Faraday's theories of electrical fields and the wave theory of light under one general mathematical formulation. Maxwell proposed that light and magnetism (until then associated with light and matter respectively) were not separate entities, but (along with electricity) were interdependent. Another scientist, Hendrick Lorentz, proposed that electrons were the connectors in this electromagnetic field. His theory opened the way for the idea of the *dual* nature of light, as both wave and particle, to gain acceptance in scientific circles. This led in turn to Albert Einstein's breakthrough conception of the electromagnetic field as the ultimate entity of the universe. Physical reality was now conceived not as material points whose changes consisted of discrete motions, but as a continuous field of electromagnetic energy.[9]

As discoveries built upon this viewpoint, scientists found that there was no way for observers to separate from the energy: the energy affected the *observer* and the observer *affected* whatever aspect of the field of energy was being studied. For example, scientists observing live specimens of flies under electron microscopes found that the rays of electrons they projected onto the flies actually changed the flies' biological structure. In the everyday world, this concept can be understood by those who work with computers. A computer artist is both an observer and creator. In the process of creation the artist can watch his or her thoughts and ideas being transferred and translated into computer images made up of beams of light. This light, now imbued with the energy of the maker, is mirrored on the screen and affects the observer/creator at least psychologically, if not physically, as some studies of electromagnetic emissions from computers suggest.

The belief in an external world independent of the perceiving subject is the basis of all natural science. Since, however, sense perception only gives information of this external world or of "physical reality" indirectly, we can only grasp the latter by speculative means. It follows from this that our notions of physical reality can never be final. We must always be ready to change these notions.

The greatest change in the axiomatic sub-structure of physics . . . since Newton laid the foundation of theoretical physics—was brought about by Faraday's and Clerk Maxwell's work on electromagnetic phenomena.[10]

—Albert Einstein

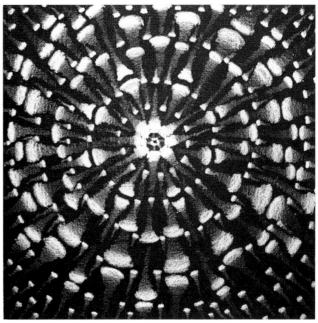

Barbara Rifkin

C. G. Jung and Western Science

Although deeply interested intellectually in Tibetan Buddhism, the yoga of Chinese Taoism, and the sacred art of the mandala, the great psychologist C. G. Jung was not a practitioner of yoga. Instead he thought of light as a metaphor for enlightenment:

The central mystical experience of enlightenment is aptly symbolized by Light in most of the numerous forms of mysticism . . . Many initiation ceremonies stage a return to the womb of rebirth. Rebirth symbolism simply describes the union of opposites—conscious and unconscious—by means of concretistic analogies. Underlying all rebirth symbolism is the transcendent function. Since this function results in an increase of consciousness . . . the new condition carries more insight, which is symbolized by more light.[11]

This fascination with light led Jung to pursue experimental work with Wolfgang Pauli, Nobel Laureate in physics. With Pauli's help, Jung began to see analogies between the interactive photons of light and the psyche. But he was quite cautious about drawing any quick conclusions:

Experience has shown that light and matter both behave like separate particles and also like waves. This paradoxical conclusion obliged us to abandon, on the plane of atomic magnitudes, a causal description of nature in the ordinary space-time system, and in its place to set up invisible fields of probability in multidimensional spaces . . . Basic to this abstract scheme of explanation is a conception of reality that takes account of the uncontrollable effects the observer has upon the system observed, the result being that reality forfeits something of its objective character and that a subjective element attaches to the physicist's picture of the world . . .

If these reflections are justified, they must have weighty consequences with regard to the nature of the psyche, since as an objective fact it would then be intimately connected not only with physiological and biological phenomena but with physical events too—and, so it would appear, most intimately of all with those that pertain to the realm of atomic physics . . . the existence of such analogies does not entitle us to conclude that the connection is already proven. We must, in the present state of our physical and psychological knowledge, be content with the mere resemblance to one another of certain basic reflections.[13]

Although acknowledging the probability that light and conscious-

Author's Note:

Today some of the most controversial theories in science propose that since energy and observer are inseparable, light and consciousness may be connected.

C. G. Jung began to explore the interrelationship between one's psyche and photons of light. Although this issue may be controversial among mainstream scientists, I have learned from experience that light and consciousness are inseparably connected and that light is primarily a spiritual manifestation of Divine Reality. This can be demonstrated in the creation of mandalas and by practice of **Raja Yoga.**

It is important to realize that this Eastern understanding of light differs both from that of Western science, which views light primarily as a material creation, and from the Jungian approach to psychology, which sees light as a subjective visual image or symbolic phenomenon accompanying inner illumination.[12]

ness were connected in some basic way, Jung mostly described light as a *symbolic representation* of mystical experiences and the emergence from psychological states of darkness. Today, however, Western scientists are discovering that light might not just *symbolically* but *actually* play a central role in all biological systems.[14] In medical science, for example, the use of light therapy for some types of depression and the use of blue light to cure rubella in infants attest to and make use of this crossover. In this way, science progresses, theory by theory. Currently, some suggestions are arising that human bodies are actually constructed and mediated by light.[15]

A Contemporary Yogic Perspective on Science and Light

In India in 1894, Swami Sri Yukteswar wrote *The Holy Science*, in which he explicitly predicted this escalating scientific ferment. According to *The Holy Science*, we have entered a new two-thousand-year cycle during which scientists will achieve a *"thorough understanding of the electricities and their attributes."*

In 1920, Mahavatar Babaji (Supreme Guru in the Indian line of masters of the Self-Realization Fellowship) sent Paramahansa Yogananda from India to the United States to advocate cultural and spiritual understanding between East and West and to initiate an exchange of their finest features. Yogananda, disciple of Swami Sri Yukteswar, founded the Self-Realization Fellowship in Los Angeles, California, where he explained cosmic creation as a dream condensation or involution of God's thought: In the process of creation, God's Absolute Nature was divided into *Absolute Nature* (vibrationless Spirit or Divine Intelligence) and *Manifest Nature,* a vibrational aspect—the sound of *Aum.* This vibrational aspect is the feminine creative nature of God as Divine Mother, or cosmic energy. This energy was divided into an infinite variety of vibratory perceptions or processes of thought. Out of pure thought came cosmic light—the tissue of the universe out of which all life forms, including the human form, emerged.

The interrelationship of light and consciousness is a vast subject, and in a book meant as a practical guide, it is possible to give only a brief synopsis of its significance. But for those readers whose interest has been sparked, I have prepared an accompanying Visual Map of Light, Sound, and Consciousness at the end of this chapter as an interpretive summary merging sacred art, science, and ancient wisdom. At a mystical level this is a picture of our soul's descent (involution) into matter or gross consciousness and our ensuing upward

It hath been said that the True State of the mind, the Thatness of all things, inseparable from the Voidness, beyond the domain of phenomena, while experiencing the thought-transcending Great Bliss, is the Primal [or Fundamental] Clear Light.

That incomprehensible, omnipresent, transcendent Divine Radiance, that illumines the All-Mind, and glows in the heart of all living things, is the Clear Light. In its glory the Bodhic Path ends.[16]

—**Seven Books of Wisdom of the Great Path**

struggle (creative evolution) to recover our authentic Self—the experiential knowing and remembering in mind, body, and soul that we are pure consciousness and one with God.

The arrows on the left side of the map point downward, representing the Eastern perspective—the involution of consciousness from subtle to gross physical states of light. On the right side the arrows point upward, representing the soul's evolution from gross states of consciousness—mirrored as the revolution and flux in Western science. There are cross-connecting arrows representing C. G. Jung's attempt to make a bridge between Eastern spirituality and Western science.

The Missing Creative Link Between East and West

The universe is a mandalic mirror—a sacred art and science of divine creative processes—manifesting as patterns of radiant rays, and ranging from spiraling galaxies, stars, and planets, to sub-atomic particles. With the aid of electron microscopes, computers, and other devices, scientists have recently been able to see the beautiful, vibrating mandalic-like patterns of atoms and molecular structures that make up the ever-changing forms of the phenomenal world.

FIG. 1.6. *Sri Yantra*, 1990, PAINTING BY AUTHOR.

Yantras are images of cosmic wholeness. This painting is based on the most famous of sacred symbols in the Hindu tantric tradition—the Sri Yantra. I have given it my own interpretation of color and luminosity. The symbol is the form equation of the sacred sound and light of *Aum.* It is mantra or sound properly intoned by a yogi, condensed into matter. It represents Self-realization and the creative involutionary and evolutionary merging of the soul back into absolute consciousness.

The mandala in the middle of the map, the sonic pattern of *Aum*, represents for me the missing creative link between East and West and between science and religion. Light, sound, and consciousness are three aspects in which we can most easily understand the unification of sacred art, Western science, and esoteric similarities within all religions. Rightly understood, the sacred art of the mandala mirroring the vibrational light of consciousness can be viewed as the creative amalgam between science and religion; inclusive of physics as well as metaphysics, it can help us to understand our own divine artistry in the unfolding patterns of light, sound, and consciousness—a process of Self-realization and ultimate healing.

Notes

[1] Lama Anagarika Govinda, *The Way of the White Clouds, A Buddhist Pilgrim in Tibet* (Boulder: Shambhala Publications, 1970), 256.

[2] Lama Yeshe, *Introduction to Tantra: A Vision of Totality* (Boston: Wisdom Publications, 1987), 31-2.

[3] H. P. Blavatsky, *Cosmogenesis*, Vol. I of *The Secret Doctrine: The Synthesis of Science, Religion, and Philosophy* (Pasadena: Theosophical University Press, 1977), 579.

[4] Paramahansa Yogananda, *The Divine Romance* (Los Angeles: Self-Realization Fellowship, 1986), 18.

[5] Paramahansa Yogananda, *Autobiography of a Yogi* (Los Angeles: Self-Realization Fellowship, 1990), 318.

[6] Ken Wilber, ed., *The Holographic Paradigm and Other Paradoxes, Exploring the Leading Edge of Science* (Boulder: Shambhala Publications, 1982).

[7] Wilber, *The Holographic Paradigm*, 160, 165.

[8] Yogananda, *Autobiography of a Yogi*, 310–311.

[9] Albert Einstein, *Essays In Science* (New York: The Philosophical Library, 1934), 47–60.

[10] Einstein, *Essays In Science*, 40.

[11] C. G. Jung's commentary in W. Y. Evans -Wentz, ed., *The Tibetan Book of the Great Liberation* (London: Oxford University Press, 1968), lxiv.

[12] David Bohm, *Wholeness and the Implicate Order* (London: Routledge, Chatman, and Paul, 1980).

[13] C. G. Jung, *On the Nature of the Psyche* (Princeton: Princeton University Press, 1973), 139.

[14] F. David Peat, *The Philosopher's Stone* (New York: Bantam Books, 1991).

[15] Robert O. Becker, *The Body Electric: Electromagnetism and the Foundation of Life* (New York: Morrow, 1985).

[16] W. Y. Evans-Wentz, ed., *Tibetan Yoga and Secret Doctrines* (London: Oxford University Press, 1958), 223–24.

EASTERN SPIRITUAL PHILOSOPHY

. . . contrary to our ordinary conceptions, light is not primarily a material creation and the sense or vision of light accompanying the inner illumination is not merely a subjective visual image or symbolic phenomena: light is primarily a spiritual manifestation of the Divine Reality illuminative and creative.

—*Sri Aurobindo*

In process of creation Divine Intelligence (Spirit) divided consciousness

ABSOLUTE NATURE (unmanifest nature or vibrationless Spirit)

↕ First differentiation of Spirit:

MANIFEST NATURE (vibrational sound—*AUM*) ↔

DUALITY CAME INTO BEING

cosmic energy-creative will,

different vibratory perceptions or processes of thought

▼

CONSCIOUSNESS and LIGHT are one and the same

except Light is a greater density

▼ ▼

Seed thoughts into Pure Thought

▼

▼ into Cosmic Light (Tissue of the Universe)

▼

▼ Specific System

Finer light-life force (Yogananda's "lifetrons")

▼

▼ Condensation of lifetrons

▼

▼ into gross atomic light

▼

▼ into photons and electrons

▼

▼ into atoms and molecules

▼

▼ into gases, heat, and liquids

▼

into various life forms

▼ ▼

into humans

▼ ▶ ▶ ↔

Merging:

**SACRED ART,
SCIENCE, AND ANCIENT WISDOM**

Unifying factors:

**LIGHT, SOUND,
AND
CREATIVE CONSCIOUSNESS**

JUNGIAN PSYCHOLOGY

▲

attempts bridge between Eastern spirituality and Western science

▲

analogies noted between consciousness and atomic physics

▲

spontaneous mandala art for healing and transformation

▲

psychic illuminations perceived as archetypal symbols

AND CONSCIOUSNESS

20ᵀᴴ CENTURY WESTERN SCIENCE

The goal of science is to augment and order our experience, and to deepen our understanding of the nature of which we ourselves are a part. —Niels Bohr

??????

CHAOS THEORY

▲

↔ **HOLISTIC CREATIVE THEORIES**
Holographic Universe Theory
Holographic Brain Theory
◄ <u>LIGHT and CONSCIOUSNESS</u> may be connected

▲

<u>DUALITIES DISCOVERED IN PHYSICS</u>

Wave/Particle duality of light
Wave/Particle duality of matter
Electron/Protons — electrical opposites
Positive/Negative magnetic Poles

▲

into various stars, planets, and life forms

▲

into gases, heat, and liquids

▲

into atoms and molecules

▲

into photons and electrons

▲

Big Bang into radiant light

▲

Big Bang Theory of Universe

▲

Theories of Relativity

▲

Theory of Electromagnetic Field as Ultimate Entity
AFTER Discoveries of FARADAY and CLERK MAXWELL

↕ **PERCEPTION of PHYSICAL REALITY**

BEFORE Discoveries of FARADAY and CLERK MAXWELL

▲

NEWTON'S SYSTEM (Physical Reality) atomistic and mechanical
Theory of Mass Motion and Gravitation
Particle Theory of Light
Heavenly bodies as material points governed by fixed laws of motion

▲

External world of matter considered separate from scientific observation

Chapter 2:

Our Bodies as Conduits of Light

[Man] has the vague intuition of a light that burns within him and which spreads out and is diffused. In this light his whole personality is concentrated and it develops around that light.

—Giuseppe Tucci, *The Theory and Practice of the Mandala*

In the creation of the universe, God's first command brought into being the structural essential: light. On the beams of this immaterial medium occur all divine manifestations.

—Paramahansa Yogananda, *Autobiography of a Yogi*

Light fills the entire universe, and there is not one region of space, however remote, that is not crisscrossed by complex patterns of electromagnetic radiation . . . Every volume of space is alive with electromagnetic radiation and therefore packed with an immense amount of data about the whole universe.

—F. David Peat, *The Philosopher's Stone*

Throughout history, the idea of a universal energy pervading all nature has been held by many Western scientific minds. This vital energy, perceived as a luminous body, was first recorded in the Western literature by the Pythagoreans around 500 B.C. They held that its light could produce a variety of effects in the human organism, including the cure of illness.

—Barbara Brennan, *Hands of Light*

The Vedanta and Sankhya [systems of Indian philosophy of which Yoga is the practical application] hold the key to the laws of mind and thought process, which are correlated to the quantum field, i.e., the operation and distribution of particles at atomic and molecular levels.[2]

—**Professor Brian D. Josephson, Nobel Laureate in Physics**

I N ESOTERIC HEALING TRADITIONS SUCH AS SHAMANISM AND yoga, healers concentrate on filling their physical bodies with prana, or life force.[1] After deep prayer, and in a state of unconditional love, the healers use the power of will and mind to direct this light through their hands to those in need of healing. The laying on of hands, therapeutic touch, loving embraces, and most physical acts of creation involve the hands as powerful ministers and architects of our thoughts.

The Healing Alchemy of Sacred Art

The exercises in this chapter prepare you to engage in an alchemy for healing the mind, body, and spirit. The exercises are designed to strengthen your will and mental powers so that they can distribute inner healing energies *(prana)* throughout your body. In the powerful mandala exercise you will make a luminous drawing of your hands. The drawing will act as a simple biofeedback device—a visual mirror to your eyes and brain—by making the invisible energies visible and more *real* to your conscious mind. As you draw, your consciousness, *prana*, physical body, and paper and pencils all will be linked in an alchemic healing process.

Healing alchemy is the magical transformation that occurs when the artist consciously focuses and directs *prana* through the body out of the hands and fingers and, along with his or her individual inspired

soul-consciousness, into corporeal materials such as pencils and paper, paints, or stone. All true sacred art is alive with the spiritual energies of the maker. If open and receptive, the maker is inwardly changed by the creative act, just as the viewer of these spiritually energized symbols is changed. As science develops more sensitive instruments, it should become possible to prove the existence of these subtle energies and to measure art-induced changes in the frequencies of light in the finished artwork as well as in the maker's physical body.

FIG. 2.1. SOUL RETRIEVAL WORKSHOP, TANAGER FOUNDATION, RENO, NEVADA.

Maja Rode

MEDITATION: *Blessing the Materials*

In traditional methods of constructing sacred and healing art, all materials are blessed before beginning. The following is a short personal ritual meant to direct the flow and blessings of Divine Light through the hands and into the materials.

Sit in an upright position on the edge of the chair, keeping your spine straight and you feet flat on the floor.

❖

Hold the two white pencils in one hand while resting that hand comfortably in your lap. Place your other hand palm down on the sheet of black paper. If you wish, play soft inspirational or sacred music in the background.

❖

Slowly take three deep breaths. On each exhalation, release all tension or negative thoughts from your mind and body. Gently quiet your breathing.

❖

Keeping your heart receptive, close your eyes, and gently focus your attention between the eyebrows at the center called the spiritual eye.

❖

In the spiritual eye, imagine your favorite saint or sage—such as Christ or Buddha—or just pure white light as being radiantly present and full of blessing for and within you.

❖

Meditate on the blessing energy. Direct it down through your neck and into your heart, feeling warmth and love. Continue directing it to all the organs, cells, and atoms in your body.

❖

Imagine the light in your body increasing and becoming incandescent.

❖

Now visualize and move this sacred light back into your heart and open to unconditional love. See the love and light flowing from your heart through your arms, hands, and fingertips, blessing the pencils and paper you are holding.

❖

Imagine this light impregnating and energizing all the atoms and molecules of these materials. When you have finished, proceed to the exercise.

❖

Nina Menrath

Materials

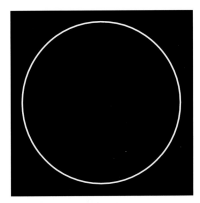

- A compass or templates (dinner plates, bowls, and large circular container covers) for tracing circles of various sizes

- A pencil sharpener

- Records or tapes of inspirational or sacred music

- Paper and pencils (see American and European Art Supplies, Chapter 1, p. 18)

Exercise: *Drawing the Outline of Hands*

1. On the large sheet of black paper draw a circle approximately 18 inches in diameter. If you do not have a compass or a large circle template, use half the sheet of black paper and don't make a circle. Either way, the drawing exercise will help develop your mind power for healing.

2. Next, use the white drawing pencil to trace the outline of your hands and arms inside the circle (or on the paper half with no circle). Draw very lightly—just enough to make the outlines visible. The outline of the hands in the accompanying renderings were made distinct to illustrate the process; do not look to them as guides as to the thickness of lines.

3. When drawing, try to capture the joy and enthusiasm of your child within. Trace at least three or more hand images, using all or part of your hand, to make the drawing dynamic. Consider overlapping two or more hand images.

4. Make sure all the lines connect either to the circle border or to some other part of the drawing. Use your imagination to connect the hands to each other and to the edge of the circle or paper. Doing this will help you with the next exercise.

FIG. 2.2 (opposite page). ILLUMINATING YOUR DRAWING.

Apply the scale-of-light technique by blending the scale *away* from the outline of your hands so that the outline disappears.

FIG. 2.3 (right). DRAWING THE OUTLINE OF HANDS.

Illuminating the Outline of Hands

The following meditation is meant to inspire you to energize the hand drawing, by helping you to develop will power through inner visioning to move the healing life force through the body and hands. After meditation you will use the scale-of-light technique learned in the first chapter to bring a sense of radiance to your line drawing. Before you begin, review the scale-of-light exercise from Chapter 1 (p. 20) and study the illustrated instructions (Fig. 2.3) for illuminating the line drawing. When you are ready, place the tracing of hands and two sharpened white pencils in front of you during the following meditation.

Exercise: *Illuminating a Drawing*

1. With that image of radiance firmly in your mind, open your eyes. Look at the drawing in front of you and decide which shapes will remain pure black and which will be illuminated. The accompanying drawings in this chapter are meant as guides only—each person doing the exercise will experience the visualization and sense of light differently.

2. Choose one area and begin to illuminate it. Starting on the outside edge of the line, apply the scale-of-light drawing technique that you learned in Chapter 1. Blend the scale of light away from the lines so that the outline of the hands disappears. Beginning at the outline of the hands, use heavy pressure to create the lightest value and gradually lighten the pressure of the pencil as you get farther away from the outline, fading the white into the black of the paper.

3. You can make a scale of light in each section of a drawing where there are enclosed lines. For example, use a scale to create a sense of light radiating off the fingertips. Stop drawing about every fifteen minutes, hang up the drawing, and stand back to examine it. From this distance, ask yourself, does the drawing have a sense of light? Did I concentrate on light radiating from the hands while I was drawing? Did I use the full scale of light—a scale going from the purest white to black? These moments of reflection will allow you to really see where you need more work so you can focus your powers of visualization and further activate the healing energies within you.

Great healers, men of divine realization, do not cure by chance but by exact knowledge. Fully understanding the control of life energy, they project a stimulating current into the patient that harmonizes his own flow of life energy. . . . Persons of lesser spiritual attainment also are able to heal themselves and others by visualizing and directing an influx of life energy to the affected part of the body.[3]

Within the gross vibration of flesh is the fine vibration of the cosmic current, the life energy, and permeating both flesh and life energy is the most subtle vibration, that of consciousness.[4]

—Paramahansa Yogananda

MEDITATION: *Bringing* Prana *Through the Hands*

Holding the two pencils in one hand, sit in an upright position on the edge of your chair, keeping your back straight, feet flat on the floor, and hands comfortably in your lap. If you wish, play soft inspirational or sacred music in the background.

❖

Slowly take three deep breaths. On each exhalation, release all tension or negative thoughts from your mind and body. Gently quiet your breath so that you are breathing slowly and softly.

❖

Keeping your heart open and receptive, close your eyes and focus your attention between your eyebrows at the center called the third eye. Imagine the *prana,* or life energy, as light coming into the back of your head at the point between your spinal column and brain (this is the medulla, the principal point of entry into the body by the *prana*).

❖

Visualize the *prana* entering into the center of your brain. Concentrate on that glowing energy and direct it down through the neck and into your heart, feeling warmth and love.

❖

Continue directing the energy to all the organs, cells, and atoms in your body. Imagine your body glowing brightly and healthily with this life force.

❖

Now visualize and move this radiant energy from the center of your heart and, feeling love, send it flowing into your arms and out your hands through the tips of your fingers. Think of pictures you might have seen of Kirlian photography. This will help you imagine more clearly the radiance coming from your hands.

❖

Then with laser-like focus, willfully direct this light into the pencils you are holding. As you grasp the pencils, imagine your inner light of consciousness impregnating all the atoms and molecules of the white pencils with *prana* and your own spiritual energies.

❖

Next, place your other hand on the black paper and with the strength of your will, move the energy from your hand into the blackness of the paper. Picture your hand tracings on the paper becoming radiantly infused with your spiritual light and life force.

❖

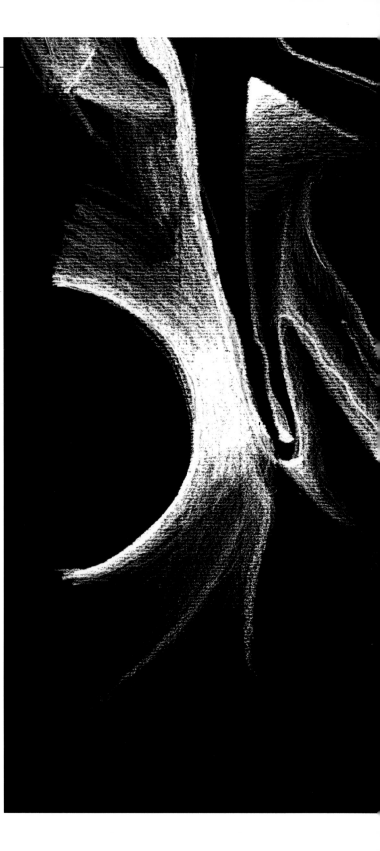

4. When you are finished, hang up your drawing and view it, allowing your conscious mind to start acting on your new awareness of the healing energies present within the body. Realize that while you have been creating an image of your hands, you have been transformed within. The more focused and concentrated you are while doing the exercise, the stronger your will becomes in moving the life force through your body for healing. *Understanding this process will help you create an alchemy of light and consciousness, merging spiritual energies with the atomic structure of your paper and pencils.*

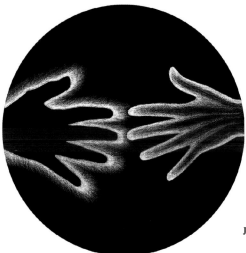

Jeanne Jerman Olson (above left), Joan Malcolm (left)

Conny Gerkn

The proposed brain model provides in large measure the mental forces and abilities to determine one's own actions. It provides a high degree of freedom from outside forces as well as mastery over the inner molecular and atomic forces of the body.[5]

—Roger Sperry, Nobel Laureate

Susan Sopcak

Key Points to Remember: *Drawing*

◆ As you draw, concentrate on intentionally willing the life force to radiate from your hands. Note that willing is different than wishing. Willing is an act of initiative.

◆ Remember to use the whole scale of light. The objective is to dissolve and blend the scale away from the outlines.

◆ If your mind wanders, bring it back to the focus of the meditation and review the inner images you saw of light radiating from the hands. Then continue drawing.

◆ While drawing, picture the tracings on the paper as radiantly infused with your spiritual light and life force.

Common Sense and Healing

You can repeat this drawing exercise as often as you like to strengthen the healing powers of your mind and will. It works by offering dynamic visual feedback of invisible energies and graphically teaching an alchemy in which the spiritual energies of the maker infuse sacred and healing art.

Where mind power has not developed sufficiently, it is not necessary to ignore the tools of traditional medicine. I speak from my own experience of battling cancer many years ago. I realized then that my own negative thinking had the power to create cancer in my body, but I also realized that my mind did not have the strength to transmute the growing cancer cells into normal healthy tissue quickly enough to prevent death. Being pragmatic, I decided to combine traditional and nontraditional methods of healing. Although I went through surgery, I also constructed healing mandalas and meditated several times a day, focusing on love and visualizing healing light penetrating the cancerous tumor. Combining these methods proved quite successful. I felt happy that I had taken sensible responsibility for my part in the cure while working in tandem with established medicine. Years later I discovered in Yogananda's teachings words of wisdom that echoed my own experience:

For erring humanity both medical and mental help are important. The superiority of the mind over material aids is undeniable, but the more limited healing power of food and herbs and drugs is also undeniable. When employing mental methods, there is no need to scorn all physical systems of cure, for the latter are the outcome of investigation into God's material laws.[7]

Unless one really knows God, he is not justified in saying that only mind exists, and that one does not need to obey health laws or to use any physical aids for healing. Until actual realization is attained, one should use his common sense in all he does. At the same time one should never doubt God, but should constantly affirm his faith in God's omnipresent divine power.[8]

Scientific research has shown that electrical activity between the left and right sides of the brain becomes coordinated during certain kinds of meditation or prayer . . . through these processes, the mind definitely becomes more capable of being altered and having its capacities maximized . . . Changed actions and a changed life will follow. The implications are exciting and even staggering . . .[6]

—Herbert Benson, M.D.,
Professor of Medicine,
Harvard Medical School

Mental power is of paramount importance as a method of healing because mind is the governor of all living cells . . . The will of man can be trained and developed to draw continuous supplies of life energy into the body to renew it indefinitely.[9]

—Paramahansa Yogananda

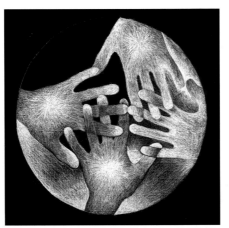

Christopher Ann Gordon

Sylvia Nachlinger

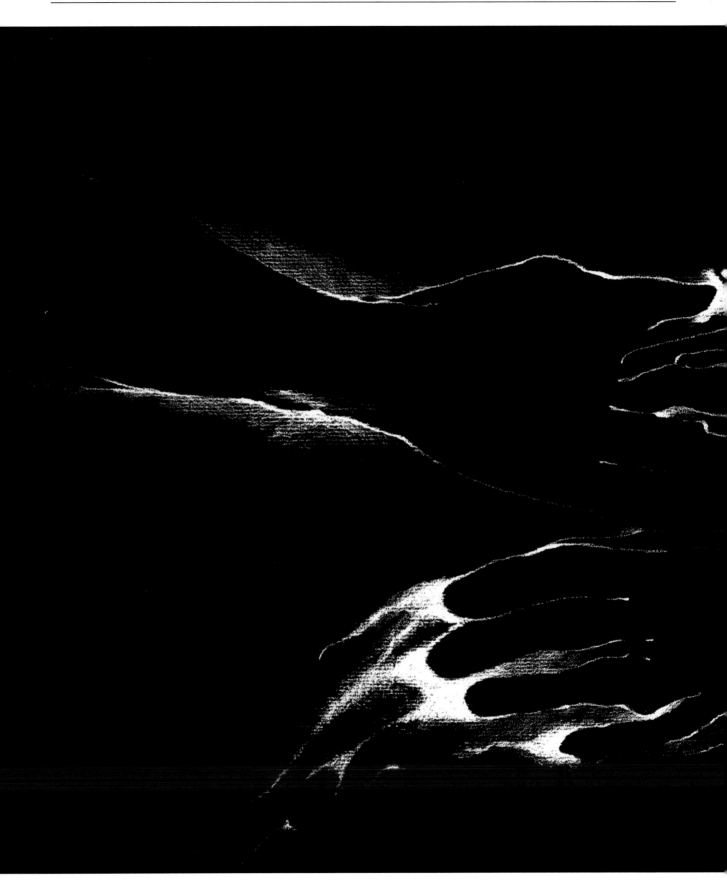

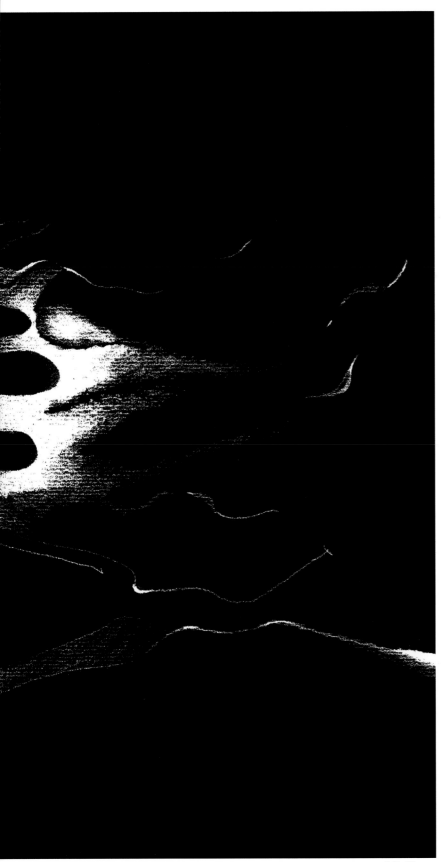

Jeffry Thomas

Summary

Review the meditation and drawing skills often as you continue in the book. The techniques in themselves are quite simple and easy to master, but our everyday consciousness, which experiences duality, continually polarizes us if we are not steeped in a disciplined spiritual practice. A divided mind keeps us believing more deeply in external reality than in the truth that we are really souls in a physical body with tremendous power to heal and feel joy. Practicing the techniques you learn here is important because they are designed to give your mind new patterns to follow, expanding consciousness from a sense of duality to the unity of pure consciousness and the perfection of your soul.

Notes

[1] Mircea Eliade, *The Two and the One* (New York: Harper & Row, 1969).

[2] Brian D. Josephson, *Self-Realization* 64 (Winter 1992), 47.

[3] Paramahansa Yogananda, *Scientific Healing Affirmations* (Los Angeles: Self-Realization Fellowship, 1990), 13-14.

[4] Yogananda, *Scientific Healing Affirmations,* 29.

[5] Roger Sperry, *Science and Moral Priority, Merging Mind, Brain, and Human Values* (New York: Columbia University Press, 1983), 39–40.

[6] Herbert Benson, *Self-Realization* 64 (Winter 1992), 49.

[7] Yogananda, *Scientific Healing Affirmations,* 32.

[8] Paramahansa Yogananda, *Man's Eternal Quest and Other Talks* (Los Angeles: Self-Realization Fellowship, 1988), 81.

[9] Yogananda, *Self-Realization* 64 (Winter 1992), 46.

CHAPTER 3:

RADIANT SYMBOLS FOR HEALING

Our Being is a brilliant pattern of energies: a spectrum of possibilities. The mystic discovers symbols . . . Symbols are windows through which we can view the Essential Nature of our Being.

—Ngakpa Chögyam, Rainbow of Liberated Energy

Symbols connected to sound, light and the Intellect are among the most profound expressions in Sufism. The Word is both a sound and a light, for the light is the meaning of the Word. The Word is as a mirror where the Divine reverberates outwardly.

—Laleh Bakhtiar, Sufi Expressions of the Mystic Quest

The visualization of light is central to tantric sadhanas and to tantric healing. One visualizes the deity radiating rays of light that enter oneself and others, completely purifying mental and physical obscurations and disease. Then the deity merges into oneself at one's heart center in the form of light. This light destroys dualistic conception, and one dwells in the state of radiant emptiness . . . One can also concentrate on healing oneself with the visualization of light.

—Terry Clifford, *Tibetan Buddhist Medicine and Psychiatry*

I N EASTERN HINDU AND TIBETAN BUDDHIST TANTRIC traditions the yogis discovered through meditation that spiritual intuition—the ability to perceive truth directly without the intermediary of the senses—could yield healing and transformative symbols. However, you need not immerse yourself in these traditions for this process to work for you. Whatever your religious affiliation or spiritual perspective, you can discover your personal healing symbols through meditation practice. This chapter covers the essence of this healing practice without the rituals that relate to specific religions or cultures. The meditation presented here will help heighten your intuitive perception so that you can spontaneously discover within yourself the symbols for constructing a healing mandala.

A hundred years ago H. P. Blavatsky stated in *The Secret Doctrine* that the third eye, or single eye of spiritual vision, now known as the pineal gland, was once fully activated in humankind but has atrophied over time as spirituality has declined.[1]

In our everyday world, the first two ways of seeing and knowing predominate. However, if we emphasize seeing with only the physical eyes and intellect, we form a limited view of who we really are and experience all kinds of dualities: good and evil, day and night, hot and cold, male and female, sickness and health. This type of seeing and

Christ, original painting by Heinrich Hofman, courtesy of Self-Realization Fellowship

The Single Eye of Spiritual Vision

We see and perceive light in various ways:

◆ through our two physical eyes, which perceive light and shadow,

◆ through the eye of reason and logic, which sees by means of the mind's light, composed of the rational truths of the intellect,

◆ and through the spiritual eye, which perceives inner light and the ultimate spiritual reality of our oneness.

Third Eye of Buddha, computer-enhanced by author

Christ echoed the yogic teachings of the East when he said:

When thine eye is single, thy whole body also is full of light . . . Take heed therefore that the light which is in thee be not darkness.

(Luke 11:34-35)

The highest spiritual center for human creation is through the third eye. The single eye of intuition, the third eye, is located between the eyebrows and inside the brain. One who is spiritually initiated by realized masters or who concentrates deeply in meditation at this point between the eyebrows can see the actual light of this third or singular eye. This golden light encircles a sphere of opalescent blue, at the center of which is a white, glowing five-pointed star.

knowing, not illumined by the integrity and clarity of spiritual perception, creates in the body/mind a sense of psychic fragmentation and separateness from others, a disease that keeps us from remembering that we are spiritual beings, primarily souls within physical bodies.

To experience wholeness and ultimate healing, we must perceive inner light and vision through the *spiritual eye*. Only when this inner way of seeing is reawakened can true healing take place, because only then can we connect with the soul. Constructing a mandala allows us to make the invisible visible by actively illuminating what Ngakpa Chögyam calls "the Essential Nature of our Being" and mirroring it back to our rational minds and brains. Like a laser beam, this focusing of the will powerfully directs healing currents of *pranic* energy to the body. From a Buddhist tantric point of view, Lama Anagarika Govinda summarizes the mandala's *mirroring* role:

> It is the first movement in the great symphonic mandala or magic circle, in which our inner world appears as sound and light, color and form, thought and vision, rhythm and harmonious coordination, visible symbol and meditative experience. This first movement . . . corresponds to the first profound meditative attitude or experience, namely "The Wisdom of the Great Mirror."

> In the light of this mirror-like wisdom things are freed from their "thingness," their isolation, without being deprived of their form; they are divested of their materiality . . . without being dissolved.[2]

You might think of the mandala as reflecting back to us the harmony and beauty of our nonmaterial reality.

Discovering a Healing Symbol

In order to *discover* a healing symbol arising spontaneously from the spiritual eye, it is important to refrain from constructing or inventing a symbol intellectually, the way graphic designers do. Instead, the goal is to become a humble receptive channel for the flow of grace and Divine Light. In this art process you become the mystic—one who discovers and reveals the spiritual essence of your being. During meditation, you consciously relinquish the ego's reinforcing notion that you are the doer or creator.

AUM —
Sacred Sound and Symbol of Inclusive Spirituality

AUM AS IT IS WRITTEN IN SANSKRIT.

Aum (Om). *The basis of all sounds; universal symbol-word for God. Aum of the Vedas became the sacred word* Hum *of the Tibetans;* Amin *of the Moslems; and* Amen *of the Egyptians, Greeks, Romans, Jews, and Christians. Aum is the all-pervading sound emanating from the . . . Invisible Cosmic Vibration; God in the aspect of Creator.*[3]

—Paramahansa Yogananda

The computer-generated image at left is made up of the core structure of the Sri Yantra. It is meant to give you an intuitional understanding of the Sri Yantra symbol as a vibrant form equation of the light and sound of *Aum*. This pattern arises when *Aum* is properly intoned as a mantra by a yogi. It is the mantra of *Aum* condensed into matter. The sound made by a human voice is, however, not the actual sound. The *actual* primal sound of *Aum* or Pure Creative Consciousness can be heard in meditation. It is the sound out of which manifest all luminous and vibrant mandalic forms of nature. Intoning the sound of *Aum* is a fundamental key to drawing luminous healing symbols for integrating body, mind, and spirit.

FIG. 3.1. SRI YANTRA.

The most holy symbol of Hindu tantric tradition, the Sri Yantra or Sri Chakra represents Self-realization and is formed from the mantric sound pattern of *Aum*. Its sacred geometry symbolizes the feminine creative aspect of sacred sound out of which the many manifestations of Divinity are mirrored back as patterns of light. However the mantric sound of *Aum* is not exclusive to either the Tibetan or Hindu tantric traditions. It is universal and can be used as a powerful healing mantra for anyone. In describing one of the essential meanings of the Sri Yantra, Sri Shankaranarayanan says:

> In manifestation, the limitless One has to limit himself in a form. The formless Great Radiance has to radiate rays of definite forms and marshal them as the various gods thus creating out of the One, the Many with distinct and distinguishable forms and features. These lines of light build the form-patterns of the gods, which are known as Yantras or Chakras . . . if one has to see the form of the Formless, the auspicious body of the Divine, the light has to be marshalled in a set pattern of radiant rays.[4]

Setting a Clear Intention for Healing

Next, it is important to have a clear intention of what needs healing. What do you wish to heal? Disease can be present in body, mind, and soul. Physical diseases are the most obvious, but fear, anger, egotism, hate, envy, lack of initiative, low self-esteem, and various other emotional disharmonies are all psychological diseases. Ignorance of the laws of life and of one's own divinity are spiritual diseases. To encompass the *cause*, not just the symptoms, in your intention to heal, be as inclusive as you can but trust your own inner guidance; for example, focus your intention on healing a physical life-threatening disease or a psychological wound such as incest. Or your intention may simply be to discover who you really are.

The Alchemy of Light and Sacred Sound

After you receive a symbol in meditation, it will enter your heart and both the symbol and your heart will be filled with the light of unconditional love. To further empower the symbol, chant the sacred sound *Aum* three times. This inclusive process of consciously invoking light and sacred sound is the *alchemical key* necessary to activate the symbol within you. This individual inner response has the ability to energize the symbols spiritually and imbue them with meaning and numinosity. Without this response, symbols are dead—mere pictures.

When you pray in meditation with clear intention for a healing symbol, you will be given one. However, many people *reject* the symbols that are revealed to them, instead drawing images their intellects and egos want to invent. When this happens it is difficult for healing to take place. The following two examples illustrate this difficulty.

Rejecting a Healing Symbol

A woman with severe back pain came to a six-day healing retreat I was facilitating. During a guided meditation, she received a healing symbol of a white dove but rejected it, saying, "No, don't give me a dove. I don't know how to draw a dove. Give me something simpler." She was shown a white lotus flower instead. She said to herself, "No, I don't want a white lotus flower, because my teacher wants us to use rainbow colors in the symbol." Later, she told the group, "I drew a rainbow-colored lotus, which became for me merely an intellectual experiment. In this process I learned that I have been rejecting the very things I have asked for, and that made me aware of how my back pain greatly increased when I followed my intellect. I began to understand

Radiant light is the function of mind, empty silence is the substance of mind. If there is empty silence without radiant light, the silence is not true silence, the emptiness is not true emptiness—it is just a ghost cave.[5]

—The Secret of the
Golden Flower

Particular symbols, or even particular interpretations of universal symbols, differ according to the various traditions. They are sensible or intelligible forms consecrated by God through revelation to become vehicles of Divine Grace . . .

The entire journey in God is a journey in symbols, in which one is constantly aware of the higher reality within things. Symbols reflect both Divine transcendence and Divine immanence; they refer to both the universal aspect of creation and the particular aspect of tradition.[6]

—Laleh Bakhtiar

that my back pain was related to my fear and to my insistence on holding onto a stuck position." The next time the woman prayed for a healing symbol, she remained humble and accepted the symbol she received. She overcame any fears she felt in constructing it. After this exercise, her back pain almost completely disappeared. By releasing her fear and opening to the power of the revealed symbol, she allowed the tense and constricted muscles of her body to relax, permitting a freer flow of healing energy.

In another incident, a woman in a healing group began to sob while working on the mandala drawing. She told me she *hated* the symbol that had come to her. I learned that this woman

Vanessa Beth Hammack

had put the symbol into her heart but refused to fill the symbol and her heart with love. She had also left out part of the symbol. I began the meditation process again, asking this woman to put all that was revealed into her heart center and fill it with love. This time the process worked, and the woman was able to get past the psychological block of hatred.

Both stories illustrate the importance of being open and receptive to the symbol you receive. It takes courage to overcome the fear associated with a symbol that seems too difficult to draw, particularly for people who have little or no art training. If you feel such fear, search in books for a picture of a dove or whatever symbol came to you and simply *trace* its outline. This way you can concentrate on the process of healing rather than worrying about trying to render your symbol realistically.

Letting Go of Ego and Competitiveness

People with traditional art backgrounds experience other problems. Many find that the ego strenuously blocks the creative flow. Academic art as it is currently taught is based on competition and the development

Jennifer Scott

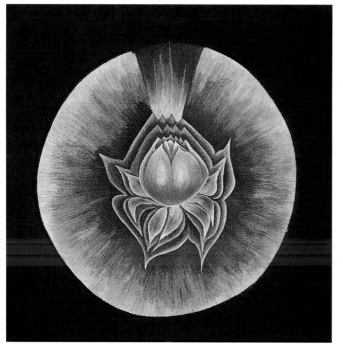

Patsy Blackstock

of a strong, distinct ego. However, the mandala process relies for its effectiveness on spiritual vision: that means opening to unconditional love, and relinquishing feelings of competition, ego, and performance anxiety. Therefore, the trained artist sometimes begins the healing exercise at a disadvantage. Often in my workshops, people with little or no training in art make mandalas that far exceed in quality and beauty those produced by trained artists. When this happens, the artists experience jealousy, envy, and sudden loss of self-confidence.

The best approach is to come to the exercise with a "beginner's mind," staying open and humble without expecting to create great art and simply doing the best you can. If you do come from a highly-skilled background, be aware that your ego may try hard to circumvent and intrude in a critical manner.

Creating a Safe and Sacred Space

Whether you do this exercise alone or in a group, create a clean, safe, and sacred workspace so that you won't be interrupted by intruders or the telephone. Light a candle or incense and visualize yourself surrounded and protected by Divine Light. You might want to have an image of your favorite saint or sage in front of you from whom to invoke help with this healing. If you have no particular spiritual practice or belief, use the candle to represent the supreme divine light within yourself. Before beginning this exercise, sit quietly and get in touch with your intention for healing. *On a piece of paper or in a journal, write this intention with as much clarity as you can.*

Bernadette Hotze

Chryssy Sibbs

Constructing a Mandala

Throughout history, mandalas have been constructed out of many materials. People often ask me if they can use materials other than black paper and colored pencils to make mandalas. The answer is yes. But I have selected black paper and white and colored pencils for the exercises in this book for two important reasons. First, it gives the reader simple materials so that anyone, regardless of drawing experience, can easily learn to create luminous healing mandalas. Second, black paper and white and colored pencils demonstrate most graphically the healing and metaphysical concepts presented in these chapters so that they can be best understood.

MEDITATION: *Blessing the Materials*

Before beginning, direct the flow of Divine Light through the hands and into the materials to bless them.

Sit in an upright position on the edge of the chair, keeping your spine straight and your feet flat on the floor. Hold the two white pencils in one hand while resting that hand comfortably in your lap. Place your other hand palm down on the sheet of black paper. If you wish, play soft inspirational or sacred music in the background.

❖

Slowly take three deep breaths. On each exhalation, release all tension or negative thoughts from your mind and body. Gently quiet your breathing.

❖

Keeping your heart receptive, close your eyes, and gently focus your attention between the eyebrows on the center called the spiritual eye. In the spiritual eye, imagine your favorite saint or sage such as Christ or Buddha—or just pure white light—as being radiantly present and full of blessing for and within you.

❖

Meditate on the blessing energy. Direct it down through your neck and into your heart, feeling warmth and love. Continue directing it to all the organs, cells, and atoms in your body. Imagine the light in your body increasing and becoming incandescent.

❖

Now visualize and move this sacred light back into your heart and open it to unconditional love. See the love and light flowing from your heart through your arms, hands, and fingertips, blessing the pencils and paper you are holding.

❖

Imagine this light impregnating and energizing all the atoms and molecules of these materials. When you have finished, proceed to the meditation *Accessing a Healing Symbol* (p. 66).

❖

Aida Ferrarone

F IG. 3.2.

The two drawings above illustrate progressive stages in illuminating a mandala. This was done by gradually building several layers and intensities of white pencil on black paper.

Susan Sopcak

Materials

- ◆ A compass or template (dinner plates, bowls, and large circular container covers) for tracing circles of various sizes

- ◆ A protractor if you plan to make precise geometric constructs within the circle

- ◆ Your written intention for healing

- ◆ A pencil sharpener and pink pearl eraser

- ◆ A notebook or journal

- ◆ Records or tapes of inspirational or sacred music

- ◆ American and European Art Supplies (see Chapter 1, p. 18)

- ◆ Some optional tools that are useful for tracing geometric or other symbolic shapes are graphic art templates made of plastic or metal. They come in a variety of sizes with various geometric shapes like diamonds, squares and ovals cut out of them.

Beth Susanne

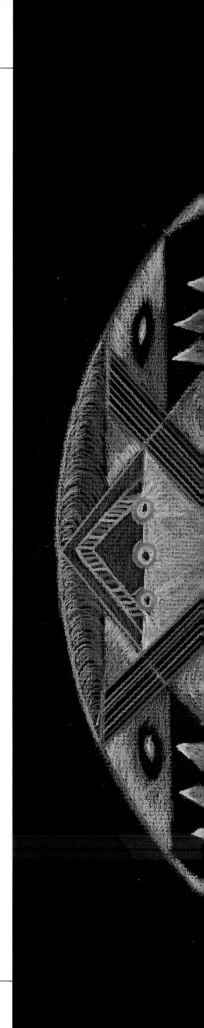

MEDITATION: *Accessing a Healing Symbol*

Once again, focus on the spiritual eye. Remember what you have written on the paper and ask with clear intention to see revealed the most perfect symbol or symbols for healing. Relax and *wait in meditative silence* for a symbol to appear spontaneously.

After receiving the symbol or symbols, humbly give thanks. ❖ Next bring the symbol into your heart and infuse it with unconditional love and brilliant blue or white light. ❖	Then, simultaneously focusing on its luminosity, activate the symbol further by chanting three times out loud the sacred sound of *Aum*. ❖ Stay a while in the meditative state, allowing the light and sound vibrations to spread as healing waves through the body/mind. ❖	When you are ready, gently come back from the meditative state and in silence write down your insights. Begin to make some small sketches of the symbols you received in your journal or notebook. ❖

. . . on the absolute plane, illness is understood to be caused by the disharmony originating from the fundamental delusion of duality and ego's self-existence. So while the relative goal of Tibetan medicine is to prevent and cure illness, its ultimate goal is the final cure of all suffering: enlightenment.[7]

—Terry Clifford

Exercise 1: *Creating a Mandala Line Drawing*

1. Begin by drawing a large circle on the black paper.

2. Next, using your sketch as reference, draw the symbol you received in meditation inside the circle. *Use very light pressure when drawing the outline of the symbol.* You may repeat and overlap a symbol more than once. You can enlarge and expand it to fill the whole circle. You may feel inspired to add other elements to the drawing as you go along; this is part of the unfolding imaginative process. Let your intuition guide you.

3. After finishing the line drawing and before beginning to illuminate it, bring into your spiritual eye the image of the mandala you have just constructed. While meditating on it with your eyes closed, imagine it radiant and alive.

4. Bring your mandala into your heart and visualize the whole of it

Susan Sopcak

pouring out from your heart through your hands and into the pencil and paper. In your mind's eye see the image as already perfectly drawn and luminous on the paper.

Fig. 3.3. Creating a Mandala Line Drawing.

These illustrations show the progressive steps for creating a luminous mandala.

Tantra challenges this unreasonably low opinion of human potential by showing us how
to view ourselves and all others as transcendentally beautiful—
as gods and goddesses in fact.

—Lama Yeshe, *Introduction to Tantra*

Exercise 2: *Bringing the Symbol to Life*

1. With that image firmly in your mind, open your eyes. Look at the drawing in front of you, and decide which areas will remain pure black and which will be illuminated with the white pencil. The examples in this chapter are meant only as guides. *To create a dynamic sensation of light some areas will need to stay dark.*

2. Choose one area and begin to illuminate it. Starting on the edge of the line, use heavy pressure to create the lightest value and gradually lighten the pressure of the pencil to fade into the black of the paper. As you did for your hand drawing in Chapter 2, blend the scale of light *away* from the lines so that the lines disappear.

3. You may draw a scale of light in each section of the mandala where there are enclosed lines. Stop drawing about every 15 minutes. Hang up the drawing, examine it from a distance, and ask yourself the following questions: Does the drawing have a sense of light? Did I concentrate on light radiating from the symbol while I was drawing? Did I use the full scale of light when drawing—a scale going from the purest white and gradually fading into black? This examination allows you to see where you need more work on the drawing.

4. When you feel you have finished, hang up your drawing and use it as a point of meditation. Then go to Chapter 4, where you will learn how to bring in other colors of light, which will add another level of meaning and healing to this drawing.

FIG. 3.4. THE BLUE MEDICINE BUDDHA, COMPUTER-GENERATED BY AUTHOR.

Tibetan physicians perform a sacred ritual to construct the Blue Medicine Buddha mandala and use it to cure illness in conjunction with other curative means such as herbs. The healer starts with mantric sounds and visualizes blue or white light streaming forth from the Medicine Buddha into the person seeking healing. This image may be used as a meditation focus to help you visualize blue healing light radiating from your third eye into your heart and flowing throughout your whole body while you are constructing your healing mandala.

According to Buddhist tantra, we remain trapped within a circle of dissatisfaction because our view of reality is narrow and suffocating. We hold onto a very limited and limiting view of who we are and what we can become, with the result that our self-image remains oppressively low and negative . . .

Many people feel that humans are little more than monkeys and that the human mind is nothing but a series of chemical reactions and electrical impulses in the brain. Such a view reduces us to lumps of matter and dismisses any notion of a higher dimension to human existence.[8]

—Lama Yeshe

Jesus answered them, "Is it not written in your law, I said Ye are gods?"

—John 10:34

"I have said, Ye are gods; and all of you are children of the most High."

—Psalm 82:6

Key Points to Remember: *Accessing Healing Symbols*

The aim of all the Tantras is to teach the ways whereby we may set free the divine light which is mysteriously present and shining in each one of us, although it is enveloped in an insidious web of the psyche's weaving.[9]

—Giuseppe Tucci

◆ Create a safe and sacred workspace surrounded and protected by divine light.

◆ Ask with clear intention to receive the perfect healing symbol. Write your intention on a piece of paper.

◆ Bless the art materials.

◆ Meditate on filling your body with divine light.

◆ Keep your attention focused in the third eye while meditating.

◆ Refrain from constructing a symbol intellectually—relax and allow it to arise spontaneously in meditation.

◆ Humbly accept the symbol that is revealed.

If you think, "I do this action," you become egotistic. Instead of being egotistic, offer everything to the Divine. If you offer everything to the Divine, there is no ego. If there is no ego you become divine . . .

To offer everything to the Divine is surrender. To give our lives to the Divine is surrender . . . Not to be egotistic is surrender. To be humble is surrender.[10]

—Mother Meera

◆ Bring the symbol into your heart and infuse it with unconditional love and brilliant light.

◆ Activate the symbol by chanting *Aum* out loud three times.

Notes

[1] H. P. Blavatsky, *Anthropogenesis*, Vol. II of *The Secret Doctrine: The Synthesis of Science, Religion, and Philosophy* (Pasadena: Theosophical University Press, 1977), 292–301.

[2] Lama Anagarika Govinda, *Creative Meditation and Multi-Dimensional Consciousness* (Wheaton, IL: The Theosophical Publishing House, 1976), 51.

[3] Paramahansa Yogananda, *Man's Eternal Quest* (Los Angeles: Self-Realization Fellowship, 1988), 467–68.

[4] Sri S. Shankaranarayanan, *Sri Chakra* (Madras: Sri Aurobindo Ashram: Dipti Publications, 1979), 6-7.

[5] Thomas Cleary, trans., *The Secret of the Golden Flower,* (San Francisco: HarperSanFrancisco, 1991), 67.

[6] Laleh Bakhtiar, *Sufi: Expressions of the Mystic Quest* (New York: Thames and Hudson, 1976), 27, 25.

[7] Terry Clifford, *Tibetan Buddhist Medicine and Psychiatry: The Diamond Healing* (York Beach, ME: Samuel Weiser, 1984), 7.

[8] Lama Yeshe, *Introduction to Tantra: A Vision of Totality* (Boston: Wisdom Publications, 1987), 41-42.

[9] Giuseppe Tucci, *The Theory and Practice of the Mandala* (New York: Samuel Weiser, 1973), 78.

[10] Mother Meera, *Answers* (London: Rider, Random Century Group, 1991), 81, 80.

Serin Eggling

CHAPTER 4:

RAINBOW COLORS AND HEALING

The inherent Buddha-nature is said to be like a diamond, indestructible, pure and empty in itself, but luminous in reflecting the manifestation of energies as rainbow light.

—Terry Clifford, Tibetan Buddhist Medicine and Psychiatry

Color and sound (music) are direct expressions of psychic experiences which cannot be grasped, defined, or expressed by the intellect . . . Thus, color reveals something that has to do with the inner nature or emotional value of form, and this is all the more so to the extent that we keep away from a mere imitation of externally visible objects and create exclusively from our inner vision or our meditative experience.

—Lama Anagarika Govinda, *Creative Meditation and Multi-Dimensional Consciousness*

Jewels also are used in healing to adjust the inner light of the subtle body . . . Gems are believed to be mines of radiations containing the power of one of seven aspects of light, the cosmic energy as manifested from the diamond-like void into rainbow light. The seven-fold spectrum of light in the rainbow represents the basic energies, forces, and quality of the manifest world.[1]

—Terry Clifford

THE RAINBOW EVOKES THE SENSE OF THE SPIRITUAL in nature. In this chapter you will learn to symbolically mirror the rainbow splendor of your soul's spiritual essence. Exercises 1 through 4 will teach you creative color blending and the logical order in which to use vibrant rainbow colors; and this, in turn, will prepare you for bringing healing colors into your black-and-white mandala drawing. These exercises are designed to help you overcome any fear you may have of using color, enabling you to enter into a spontaneous and creative exploration of color and its enriching luminosity.

Rainbow Light

In many cultures, the rainbow is associated with the metaphysical sciences, occult healing, and divinity. In Genesis, the rainbow is a sign of God's covenant and spiritual protection. And in Tibetan yoga, the purified astral or subtle body of an enlightened yogi is called the rainbow body. According to Hindu and Buddhist teachings, human beings have three bodies of light—the gross outer physical body, a subtle body of light known as the astral body, and the causal body. Through high spiritual attainment, self-realized yogis have been known to purify the astral body and transmute the gross physical body into what Tibetan Buddhists call the rainbow body, or Body of Glory. In this Body of Glory, master yogis are said to exist for eons, working at will on any level of reality within the universe. An example of such masters are Babaji and his sister Mataji, as recounted by Paramahansa Yogananda in *The Autobiography of a Yogi.*

Until recently, fraudulent practices by chromotherapists and the taboo among scientists against any serious investigation of the occult have discouraged Western science from contemplating the effects of light. But through the new science of photobiology, the medical establishment has begun to study the strange effects of visible and invisible light and color on humans and other living organisms.

Western science has long understood that the rainbow is but a tiny part of the vast electromagnetic spectrum of rays. Without special devices, our eyes can see only the white light portion of that spectrum. Science is beginning to discover that the visible rainbow and invisible rays, such as x-rays, radium, and microwaves, are interwoven to create our physical reality. Research now suggests that many rays affect our vision, bodies, minds, and all functions on Earth.

We are only just beginning to comprehend the potency of these multiple rays. Advanced technology tells us that they can be harnessed to heal or to destroy. To protect ourselves as we learn and experiment, it is important for us to integrate the *subjective* knowledge that yoga teaches with the *objective* insights of Western science. We have much to learn about the interrelationships of mind, body, and light. It only makes sense that we draw from *all* sources of potential knowledge. The short overview below is my attempt to weave together what we know and are beginning to intuit about the interweavings of light, color, sound, and consciousness.

Rainbow Color: *East and West*

In the Hindu tradition, each of the seven chakras—the esoteric centers of life and consciousness—is associated with a specific astral sound and with one of the colors of the rainbow spectrum. Through meditation on the inner vision of the third eye, advanced yogis are able to hear the sounds and see auras and the more subtle rainbow lights that constitute the astral body and chakras. Through esoteric investigation and by developing the powers of the mind, advanced yogis have discovered many healing properties of light and sound and are able to direct healing colors to both the astral and physical bodies. Tibetan Buddhist physicians, for example, send various curative rays into both people requesting healing and medicines prepared for them. One of the incarnations of the Divine Mother from India, Mother Meera, considers colors of light as sacred manifestations of divine beings:

. . . they came to a place where they could see from above a line of light, straight as a column, extending right through the whole heaven and through the earth, in color resembling the rainbow, only brighter and purer . . . and there, in the midst of the light, they saw the ends of the chains of heaven let down from above: for this light is the belt of heaven, and holds together the circle of the universe . . .[2]

—Plato

Golden and white lights are the lights of Paramatman . . . other lights belong to Avatars, Gods and Goddesses. The light of Durga is red and is characterized by power. The blue light is Krishna and is the light of knowledge and love. Violet light is for physical health. Green is the color of the life force in the material world. Orange is the color of sacrifice, the color of sannyasins [one who renounces worldly pursuits for a life dedicated to God].[3]

In meditating on and drawing mandalas, you will be gaining access to the healing colored light within yourself, just as Tibetan yogi physicians use the power of their minds to visualize and direct the healing blue light of the Medicine Buddha to their patients. This methodology differs from the Western medical approach to color healing. Although Western scientists have discovered some healing properties of light—for example, that blue light from a mechanical source can sometimes cure a baby with rubella—so far their focus has been on *external* light rather than the integrating light source within.

Symbolic Color Systems

In my workshops, participants who sincerely meditate and ask with intention to receive healing colors find that colors for a particular symbol arise spontaneously within the third eye. The drawing exercises that we do together mirror back these colors through the medium of rainbow-colored pencils. Many esoteric systems use colors symbolically—not just to heal the physical body but to integrate body, spirit, and the greater reality. However, you don't have to abandon your culture or bind yourself to the imagery of another to do the same.

Lama Ngakpa Chögyam clarifies the necessity of achieving an authentic system of color not from external sources but from one's own personal visual experience:

There are many systems of colour . . . in the world and although there are similarities between them they are mainly not externally aligned with each other. This, however, is no cause for conflict unless we make it so, because each system (if it is an Authentic system Realized through Direct Visionary Experience) functions perfectly within its own context.[4]

In the Tibetan tantric tradition, for example, white is the color of water and is associated with the East and with anger and clarity. In North America, the Plains Indians associate white with the north—with the buffalo and wisdom. The Irish of old assigned black to the north and white to the south. The Mayans of Yucatan chose white for the north and yellow for the south. The Apache, Cherokee, Chippewa, Creek, and Zuni Indians assigned colors to the four directions, but those colors differed from tribe to tribe. By meditating deeply and trusting your intuition, you will find a unique personal color system that works for you.

In contrast, Western science views light and color as being separate from consciousness and having no inherent spiritual essence or divine qualities. According to Western physics, the beauty of the rainbow is revealed when white light is refracted through a prism into individual spectral colors—magenta-red through red-orange, yellow, green, turquoise-blue, and blue-violet.

In 1666, Sir Isaac Newton discovered this spectrum of pure colors. He found that purple does not exist independently but forms when the magenta-red and blue-violet ends of the spectrum are brought together. This led him to chart the colors of visible light in the form of a circle called a *color wheel*.

Modern science has discovered that light behaves both as a

Anne Herrick

Barbara Rifkin

wave and as a particle. The wave theory of light is applied to color television and computer screens. The phosphorous particles that coat our TV and computer screens emit colors of rainbow light when stimulated with electron guns. If you work on computers you might have heard the term "RGB" mode. This represents the *primary colors* of light—a reddish-orange (R), green (G), and blue-violet (B)—which, when added together in varying intensities, produce a rainbow spectrum of colorful and luminous TV or computer images. I used a computer with a color monitor to create the image on the cover of this book. Hence, this image was created by using the wave theory of light and its primary colors "RGB." But in order for that image to be printed in *ink* onto paper, the *particle theory* of light was used.

Artists' Pigments, Printers' Inks, and Rainbow Color

The particle theory of light for artists' pigments and printers' inks takes into account the dense atomic and molecular structure of these materials, composed of photons and electrons, which interact with visible light. It was a hundred years after Isaac Newton's discovery before a color theory for pigments was developed. In 1731, French scientist J. C. Le Blon theorized that the primary colors for pigments were red, yellow, and blue. This theory was applied immediately to painting, printmaking, and engraving. However, it was not until 1766 that a well-organized color circle emerged from Le Blon's theory.

It was in our own century that American colorist Herbert Ives introduced turquoise-blue (called *cyan* in the print industry) and magenta-red pigment colors as primary colors for the pigment color wheel for artists. Cyan blue, yellow, and magenta are now considered the primary colors of inks, which are used along with black to produce a rainbow spectrum of colors. Based on the present color theory for pigments, the computer-generated image of this book's cover was reconverted from light emissions in the monitor to the denser molecules of primary color printers' inks.

Most people in the arts who use pigments have been trained to use a reddish-orange and an ultramarine-blue as primary colors of red and blue. However, I have found Ives' primary colors—magenta-red, turquoise-blue, and yellow—to be much more vital as primary pigment colors. They inject an intense vibrancy into the pigment spectrum. You will be using this spectrum for the exercises in this chapter.

Scientists have discovered that pigments reflect about two-thirds of the visible spectrum. The color reflected depends on each pigment's molecular composition. A pigment that *appears* to our eyes as the color magenta is really a reflection of combined wavelengths. According to physics, although a magenta-colored pencil *looks* magenta, the color is an illusion. The pigment in the pencil is absorbing most of the medium waves of the white-light spectrum and reflecting back the rest of the waves from its surface to give it its color. Said another way, the color that appears to our eyes is a dance of duality between light *waves* and atomic *particles*.

Experiencing the Joy of Color

At an atomic level, colored pencils are pulsing with energy—both absorbing inwardly and reflecting outwardly. Each pencil is a vibrating molecular structure, one that can be affected by your particular spiritual energies. The following exercises will teach you how to *reflect* back rainbow colors in an ethereal way. As you enter into and experience the joy of color, you will automatically be drawn toward creative color blending—merging the material science of color mixing with the alchemy of light and consciousness. This integral perspective will yield many ways of healing with color and expressing the multi-faceted rainbow nature of your soul. *Before you begin the exercises, bless all your materials as you did in Chapter 2, p. 41.*

Aida Ferrarone

Myra Herman

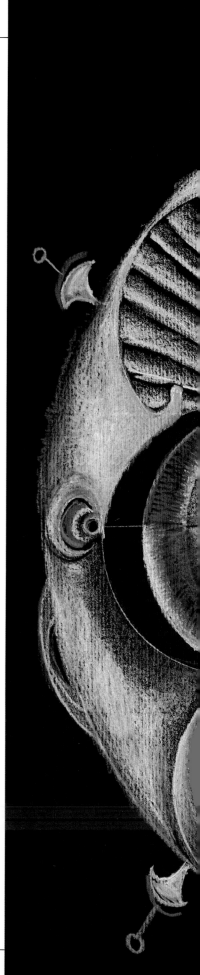

Sheri Gillette Espar

Native American motif

Aztec calendar

Materials

◆ 1 high-quality, hand-held or electric pencil sharpener

◆ 1 pink pearl eraser

◆ 1 large sheet of black pastel paper (see "Materials," Chapter 1, p. 18)

◆ Tapes of inspirational music

◆ Berol Prismacolor or Berol Karisma Colour Pencils

You will need the following eight pencils for exercises 1 through 6:

938 White (2 each)	935 Black
905 Aquamarine	918 Orange
930 Magenta	913 Spring Green or Green Brice
916 Canary Yellow	932 Violet

Once you have completed the exercises, you may wish to experiment freely with the following colors. Most people enjoy adding these beautiful hues to their box of colors:

902 Ultramarine Blue	904 Light Blue	956 Light Violet
992 Light Aqua	934 Lavender	929 Pink
707 Peacock Blue	PC 1006 Parrot Green	998 Bright Violet
923 Scarlet Lake	903 True Blue	910 True Green
933 Blue Violet	944 Process Red	

Susan Sopcak

Exercise 1: *Drawing Primary Colors as Scales of Light*

For this exercise you will need your art materials and the following four pencils: 905 Aquamarine, 930 Magenta, 916 Canary Yellow, and 938 White. The exercise will guide you in experiencing each of the primary colors as radiant light by creating a scale of light for each one.

1. Create a scale of light using the white pencil.

2. Create a scale of light for each color. For each scale, move smoothly from pure color through a gradual fading into the blackness of the paper. You may have to go over the scale a few times to smooth out the transition from color into black.

Exercise 2: *Primary Rainbow Colors Over White Pencil*

This exercise uses the same primary colors but teaches you how to create a rainbow effect by overlapping and blending each color over white pencil (Fig. 4.2). The object is to discover how blended color looks over a scale of white pencil on black paper. Black and white are the most extreme and contrasting values of light. All other colors of the rainbow fall in a range between these two.

A blend of two primary colors is called a secondary color. For example, blending magenta and yellow creates various orange and red-orange colors. As you create a scale of light, some of the black paper will show through the layer of pencil color. When this happens, an optical blend of color plus black will be reflected back to your eyes. Technically, this mixture of black plus color is called a *shade*.

FIG. 4.1 (upper left). PRIMARY COLORS AS SCALES OF LIGHT.

This color wheel was created using the three primary colors of pigments: magenta, aquamarine, and yellow. The white triangle in the center indicates how the rainbow emerges out of white light and how each of the three primary colors overlaps to create a full spectrum. The equilateral triangle, with each of its sides representing one color, expands into a geometric pattern of energy, and begins to convey the sacred geometry of light, sound, and consciousness.

Below the color wheel, each of the three primary pencil colors was drawn as a separate scale of light—proceeding from intense layering of pigment to a gradual fading into darkness. This is the first exercise you will do.

Susan Sopcak

FIG. 4.2 (above). PRIMARY RAINBOW COLORS OVER WHITE PENCIL.

As you experiment, bring a meditative focus to these color exercises. It will help you to release fear and to experience the joy of color blending expressed through sacred geometry. This first exercise teaches you to blend primary colors to create a rainbow, using the equilateral triangle as a template.

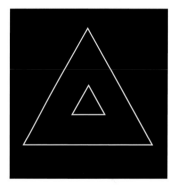

FIG 4.2A (right). DOUBLE TRIANGLE.

This illustration shows a small equilateral triangle inside a large equilateral triangle which you will draw in white for Exercise 2.

FIG 4.2B (lower right). HINDU YANTRA.

This Hindu Yantra shows the triangle as a symbol of sacred geometry. In the Hindu tradition, the two triangles represent the *marriage* of the masculine and feminine aspects of Consciousness. Pointing upward, the triangle represents the masculine principle of Supreme Consciousness. Pointing downward, it represents the feminine principle of creation (the Divine Mother) manifesting in nature as various patterns of light, sound, and consciousness.

Michael Mitchell

When you blend white with a color, it mixes visually into a pleasing pastel. White plus color is called a *tint*. You can achieve the greatest range of light values by skillfully using colored pencils over and under white pencil on black paper and by allowing some of the black of the paper and black pencil to show through darker areas of color.

While doing the exercises, remember to hold to the consciousness that the pigments are in reality both reflecting and absorbing light.

1. Begin by drawing a small equilateral triangle inside a large equilateral triangle in white pencil on your black paper.

2. On each side of the small triangle, use your white pencil to create a scale of light gradually blending it back to the large triangle—intense white fading to black.

3. On each side, blend one of the three colors over the white, but this time, begin with very light pressure over the most intense white area and gradually increase the pressure and amount of pigment as you extend the scale into the black of the paper.

4. Do not press the pencil heavily when you blend color over the white. With a light touch, blend it on top of the white or you will lose the white, which is the lightest value of all the colors. By minimizing the color you put over the white and by layering white over the colors, you can create soft, luminous, pastel colors. In this next part you will begin with color scales starting on the sides of the large triangle.

5. On one side line of the large triangle blend a scale of magenta working from intense color gradually blended over black and with very light pressure fading to soft color over white. Imagine the color as radiant magenta light that is glowing and alive.

6. Choosing another side, do the same procedure for yellow, blending and overlapping it with the magenta to create orange.

7. Then blend the aquamarine on the last side, overlapping and blending it with the yellow and the magenta.

8. In order to achieve the secondary colors of greens, oranges, and violets, you will need to overlap and blend each of the primary colors where they meet the corners of the triangle.

Exercise 3: *Creating a Rainbow with Primary and Secondary Colors*

In the second exercise, you learned to create secondary colors—those colors created by blending or mixing two primaries together. In the following exercise, you will add three manufactured, secondary-colored pencils to the palette of primary colors used in Exercise 1, p. 84. Now you will use six pencils plus white: Aquamarine, Magenta, Canary Yellow, Orange, Violet, and Spring Green or Green Brice. This fuller palette will help you achieve more subtle color effects.

1. Begin by drawing a small hexagon inside a larger one in white pencil, on your black paper.

2. On each side of the small hexagon, use your white pencil to create a scale of light, gradually blending it back to the larger hexagon—intense white fading to black.

3. Using the diagram as a guide, blend the colors just as you did in Exercise 2. The difference here is that you now blend between a manufactured primary color and a manufactured secondary color to create a third color blend. See Fig. 4.3 for the color placement necessary to create the logical order and reflection of rainbow colors.

Susan Sopcak

4. On one side of the large hexagon, blend a scale of magenta, working from intense color gradually blended over black to soft color over white.

5. On the side next to it follow the same procedure using orange, blending and overlapping it with the magenta to create an in-between color—reddish-orange.

6. Then blend the yellow next to the orange, overlapping and blending them together.

7. Continue on until you have blended and overlapped all six colors.

FIG. 4.3. CREATING A RAINBOW USING SIX COLORS.

In the third exercise, you will use the sacred geometry of the hexagon as a template to blend the primary and secondary colors of the rainbow. On each side of the small hexagon, use your white pencil to create a scale of light, gradually blending it back to the larger hexagon—intense white fading to black. By creating these overlapping patterns of white light, you will see a radiant six-pointed star appear.

Exercise 4: *Adding Luminous Color Effects*

Because color is spiritual in nature and our response to it emotional, by enhancing a symbol with luminous color, you can greatly intensify its power to effect inner transformation. If you were to color the same symbol three different ways, each change would alter the symbol's psychological impact. Fig. 4.4 demonstrates this phenomenon. Each of the color symbols has its own unique feeling. As you study these examples, pay attention to their emotional and spiritual effects. On the left side of each row the colors of the symbol look flat in tone. This flat or solid use of color tends to convey a static or dead quality. The coloring of the symbols on the left was not blended over white in order to illustrate the static effect of solid color. But the symbols on the right appear radiantly alive. Because color was used here to represent spiritual light, these symbols captivate our vision and affect us emotionally, conveying a sense of inner light and the spiritual aspects of nature. Technically, this effect was refined with black and white pencils. The result is a broad range of light values blended and layered together with the rainbow colors. The color bars on the right illustrate additions of white to each of the colors and additions of black pencil blended in with the white pencil.

Notice that the two rows of symbols are coded differently. The color coding in the top row indicates that the symbols were colored with the three primary colors only. The coding in the bottom row indicates that these symbols were colored with both primary *and* secondary colors.

FIG. 4.4. ADDING LUMINOUS COLOR EFFECTS.

A symbol can be colored in various ways. The black-and-white illustrations next to each row of colors are meant to show that even though the outline of a symbol remains the same, artist Susan Sopcak applied the scale of white *differently* in each symbol. Color is also affected by the way the white is applied.

The two rows of symbols are coded differently. In the top row the symbols were colored with the three primary colors plus white and black. The symbols in the bottom row were colored with eight colors—the primary *and* secondary colors plus black and white. The color bars on the right, underneath each row, illustrate a scale of light, showing additions of white pencil to each of the colors and additions of black pencil blended in with the white pencil.

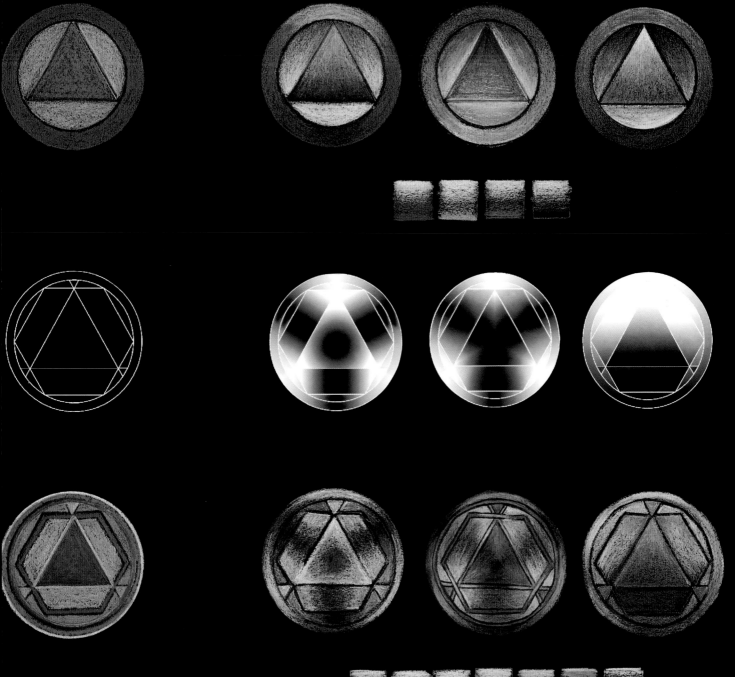

We have to try to reveal that Light
which is hidden in us as a bud. It
must blossom like a flower. In all
things everywhere, in all beings, the
Light is hidden, and it must be
revealed . . . I want the Paramatman
Light to blossom everywhere.[5]

—Mother Meera

For this exercise, you will need your primary colors and secondary colors plus black and white.

1. Begin by drawing a small circle. Inside the circle, draw a simple geometric shape, such as a triangle. You can draw the same symbol two or three times. Then apply primary colors to the symbols to see how coloring them differently affects the feeling coming from the symbol.

2. Go on to experiment with a different symbol. Draw it two or three times. Then color the symbols by applying primary and secondary colors plus white and black. Study Fig. 4.4 to see how white and black pencil and color can be used creatively to increase radiance.

Applying Healing Colors to Symbols

Having completed the four preliminary exercises, you have immersed yourself in the qualities of luminous color. Now you will integrate your new familiarity with the power of color into the healing mandala you created in Chapter 3.

People often tell me that they have chosen colors even before they begin the meditation explained below. You may find that you have this same tendency. However, to avoid allowing your ego or intellect to make your color choices, it is better to enter deep meditation and ask with intention that the best colors for your symbol be revealed to you. The colors people receive in meditation are usually

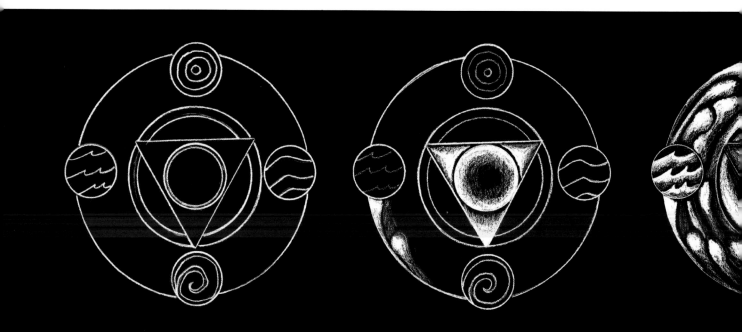

quite different from those they would have chosen without meditation.

One of my workshop students, for example, received the complimentary colors of violet and yellow to use in the drawing. Normally this man actively disliked these colors, but as the process unfolded, he began to trust the intuitive process and emphasized violet and yellow in the drawing along with all the other colors of the rainbow. The result was a beautiful, fully realized mandala. Colors that are spontaneously revealed are sometimes meant as challenges to help us penetrate energy blocks in the physical or astral body.

All the answers are within you, but meditation is necessary for gaining access to these higher states of soul-inspired intuition. Our everyday consciousness does not always know what the soul knows and if we let it, would guide us toward that which is easiest or most familiar, rather than toward that which challenges us to go through transformation. For this reason, I stress the importance of meditating to discern symbols and colors.

FIG. 4.5. PROCESS FOR COLORING A MANDALA.

These illustrations by Susan Sopcak review the procedures for coloring a

mandala with radiant color. The first image is the original, dynamic black-and-

white drawing. The fourth image shows how Susan began to blend color over

the white pencil and black paper on her original drawing. The last image is that

same drawing completely colored.

Susan Sopcak

Meditation: *Blessing the Materials*

Before you begin bless the materials as you did in Chapter 2, page 41.

MEDITATION: *Accessing Healing Colors*

Before beginning, place your black-and-white mandala and all the colored pencils in front of you. If you don't see any colors during meditation, trust the energy you feel during the meditative process. This energy will guide you intuitively to select the appropriate colors once you have finished meditating.

Once again, focus on the spiritual eye. Imagine your mandala drawing in the spiritual eye. Ask with intention that the perfect colors to use with this symbol be revealed.

❖

Relax and *wait in meditative silence* for colors to appear spontaneously within the symbol.

❖

After receiving the colors, humbly give thanks.

❖

Next, bring the colorful glowing symbol into your heart and infuse it with unconditional love.

❖

Then, simultaneously activate the luminous symbol further by chanting the sacred sound *Aum* three times out loud.

❖

Stay a while in the meditative state, allowing the light and sound vibrations to spread as healing waves of color throughout the body/mind.

❖

When you are ready, gently withdraw from the meditative state, and in silence begin coloring your mandala.

❖

Exercise 5: *Coloring the Mandala*

People often wonder how to begin coloring. My suggestion is to have all your pencils sharpened and within easy reach. Then just begin, starting anywhere on the paper as the spirit moves you. You might try playing sacred music. It can help you relax and free you from a sense that you are the doer. Keep in mind that as you surrender to the spontaneity of the energies flowing through you, the joy and healing affects of color will be revealed.

1. Bless the materials before beginning. Let go of fear and open your heart to unconditional love.

2. As you color the symbol, give your imagination free play, allowing yourself to open to the child-like joy of bringing the other rainbow colors into your drawing. If you feel stuck at any time, begin to meditate again and ask for help. Remember that meditation gives you the seed idea for coloring your mandala. When this seed is watered with devotion and love, it will flower into a luminous pattern infused with the healing qualities of light and color.

3. Remember to use color as a scale of light in combination with white and black.

4. Meditate on color as a spiritual energy while working.

5. Any time you feel uncertain about coloring, go back into meditation and ask for help.

6. Every so often while you are working on the drawing, hang it up and look at it from a distance. This will give you a new perspective and will help you to see areas where you want to make more value changes, so that it becomes truly alive and more luminous.

7. When you look at the drawing, squint at it with your eyes half-closed. Does the drawing look gray? If so, look to see if you have enough deep, dark areas contrasted with areas that are very bright and light.

8. How will you know when you have completed the process of coloring? When you no longer have any doubts that you could make it any better. Do not stop coloring if you fear you will ruin your mandala if you continue—that fear is a sign that you are not finished.

   The mandala process brings up and mirrors all the fears that we need to overcome. Have courage to go past this fear of failure and take the risk to color guided by your heart and soul. Doing a series of mandalas is one way to overcome fear and continue the healing process. Many people who use the mandala for healing create a series of them. Mandalas act as a visual journal of our spiritual journey from fear and entrenchment in darkness to embracing and expressing the radiance of the soul's true nature.

Beth's Story of Healing and Integration

Beth Susanne was first introduced to the mandala during one of my retreats. As she had no previous formal training in the visual arts, she came with a humble beginner's mind. Her intention was to heal from intense psychological pain she had experienced during a divorce. At base, she was on a quest to discover who she really was. In looking back to that retreat, she said:

The experience of creating my first mandala was the single most healing and validating experience of my life. Every cell of my body absorbed the impact of seeing and owning who I was. I realized that if I could create something that beautiful and powerful, having believed previously that I wasn't creative, then it followed that the other boundaries I'd constructed about my life and limiting beliefs I had about myself were also false.

During the guided meditation, Beth saw images spontaneously arise within her inner vision. With great inspiration, she incorporated these into her mandala:

Once I began to draw, I couldn't stop. I had a ferocity of focus and a flow of evolving creativity as I'd never experienced before in my life. The design took me all day to do and radiate with white. I didn't begin to apply color to the symbol until five o'clock in the evening and then I continued to work on it until one o'clock in the morning. As I was pulled towards completing my mandala, I kept having flashes of the urgency you have in labor (without the pain) to keep going until the baby comes out whole and healthy.

That night, the result had so powerful an impact on me that it is difficult to describe. For the first time in my life I felt a flow of energy rushing through me with such intensity from the top of my head through my body and out of my feet, that when I went to bed I felt acutely aware of all things as if magnified and slowed down. The moonlight, the density of the shadows and darkness of the night, the birds singing, the distant roar of traffic, my roommate's even breathing while asleep—everything was not only heard or seen, but felt as a part of me—as if where I ended the outside world began. No boundary existed—we were all one breathing, energy-filled being.

A Mandala for a Special Friend with Cancer

A specially created mandala is a wonderful and loving gift for someone who is in need or in crisis. Making a mandala for a person's spiritual, mental, or physical healing by praying and pouring love into it focuses healing energy both for the giver and the receiver. This gift of healing art can then be hung as a meditative symbol wherever the recipient can use it.

After her original retreat, Beth Susanne created twenty mandalas over a nine-month period. One of these was for a friend who had breast cancer. Referring to the experience, she said:

I poured all the love and intensity of caring I felt for my dearest friend who was so ill from breast cancer in the meditation for her symbol. I felt an enormous need to do something concrete for my friend that would help her heal, something from my inner core that would reflect the intensity of love and affection I felt for her.

So I asked for a symbol (while meditating in the third eye) that would radiate her highest healing energy wrapped in my love and I saw the Jewish star, the blue

Beth Susanne

healing light, the birds flying to freedom, the lotus suspended but still integrated into the whole— all wrapped in my magenta heart. I felt the same urgency and connectedness to all things that I experienced in creating all my mandalas.

I wanted to create a symbol which would reflect her vibrancy, warmth, caring, and joyous celebration of life. It also needed to reflect my deeply-felt appreciation of who she is as a spiritual being. She is one of those rare beings who really sees

me, hears me, and values me for who I am at my core. All of these feelings I wanted to put into the mandala so that she would have that loving energy around her, reflected back to her for her to see and feel every day as she heals.

MEDITATION: *Creating a Mandala for Another Person*

Use the same procedure as in Chapter 3 for gaining access to a healing symbol by focusing in your the third eye and quieting your breath. This time, however, bring to the eye the image of the person for whom you are making the healing gift.

While focusing in the third eye, expand your heart with unconditional love for that person and ask his or her permission to make this healing symbol.

❖

Ask to have revealed the perfect symbol for this healing, whether spiritual, mental, or physical. If you ask for the best symbol for the person's highest good, you will be avoiding your ego's tendency to control the direction of the healing gift and allowing divine grace to flow through you.

❖

Bring the symbol into your heart and chant *Aum* on it three times. In the third eye, see the illumined symbol being sent to the person whose gift it will be.

❖

After meditation in which you hold the person lovingly in your thoughts, bless the materials and begin to draw the symbol in white on black paper.

❖

When it is time for color, again take the symbol into the third eye and during meditation ask for the perfect colors for this symbol to be revealed.

❖

It is important to do this process with as much love, devotion, and meditative focus as possible. To color the symbols, simply follow the steps given in the preceding exercise.

❖

I ask people to maintain silence during the retreats—except for questions that pertain to the process. This helps to keep the energies focused and to silence the chatter of the intellect, which can impede the process by dissipating the creative energies. However, at the end of a retreat I ask people to display their mandalas and if they wish they can at that time also verbally share what is in their hearts. But the most powerful sharing is in the visual image of the mandala itself as a wordless reflection of the soul's essence. The symbol serves as a new way to reveal who its creator really is. Beth puts it this way:

After forty years of searching to find out who Beth was, I finally knew. I saw my own and everyone else's mandalas as wonderful unique expressions of the individual's life-force. My mandala in front of my eyes revealed my intensity, vibrancy, power, warmth, strength. I knew that here in concrete, visual form, outside myself, for any—and everyone—to see, was who I was. I didn't need to say anything, explain anything, fill someone in on my background. Now all they had to do was to take one look and they would know who I was.

Summary

Our sense of separateness and fragmentation is deep. By doing a series of mandalas, as Beth did, we can give the brain and mind more accurate energy patterns of who we really are: numinous, whole, harmonious, and beautiful souls reflected as rainbow patterns of light and sound. Dr. Michael Flanagin's Afterword to this book recounts two such unfoldings in fascinating detail: the story of C. G. Jung and his personal experiences with mandalas, a well as a dramatic, fully-documented case history of one of Jung's patients.

Notes

[1] Terry Clifford, *Tibetan Buddhist Medicine and Psychiatry* (York Beach, ME: Samuel Weiser Inc., 1984), 81.

[2] Plato, *The Republic: Book X* (Roslyn, NY: Walter J. Black Inc., 1942), 489.

[3] Mother Meera, *Answers* (London: Random Century Group, 1991), 40.

[4] Ngakpa Chögyam, *Rainbow of Liberated Energy* (Dorset: Element Books, 1986), 44.

[5] Mother Meera, *Answers*, 17.

Chapter 5:

Healing Our Relationships

I was seeing in a sacred manner the shape of all things in the Spirit, and the Shape of all Shapes as they must live together like one being and I saw the sacred hoop of my people was one of many hoops that made one circle wide as daylight and as starlight and in the center grew one mighty flowering tree to shelter all the children of one mother and one father and I saw that it was holy.

—Black Elk, Sioux holy man and
keeper of the Sacred Pipe

When Indians say that we are all related to all things, we mean that all races have the same Mother, Mother Earth, and we are all brothers and sisters . . . If all things on earth are from Mother Earth, related through her, and sustained from her, there is no basis for prejudice.

—Ed McGaa, Eagle Man, *Mother Earth Spirituality*

THROUGH EMPOWERING THOUGHT, IMAGINATIVE vision, and focused energy of desire and will, together we create our world. However we may want to deny it, we are each responsible for beauty and harmonious relationships as well as disease and ecological crisis. The Earth has become a global village in which human beings are instantly and intimately connected by the "miracle" of telecommunications technology. Through this information network, the images contained in humanity's collective consciousness are constantly mirrored back to us in television, film, radio, newspapers, and computer networks. Like a shattered, smoky mirror, those sources reflect mostly dismal images of war, ecological rape, violence, hate, greed, jealousy, and racial and gender prejudice. If we accept this as the only true reflection of our way of being with one another and with the Earth, then we will continue to create from this diseased state of consciousness. But, as the mandala itself can show us, there is another way.

Putting the Pieces Back Together

By revisioning, and therefore changing, our consciousness, all of our personal and global relationships can be brought into harmony. The greatest challenge facing each of us is to take personal responsibility for living in harmony with all life forms and understanding the delicate web of connections between all life and the Earth. To see with the clear mirror of our soul's vision the underlying truth of the light

. . . in accord with the Eastern conception, the mandala symbol is not only a means of expression, but works an effect. It reacts upon its maker. Very ancient magical effects lie hidden in this symbol . . . the magic of which has been preserved in countless folk customs.[1]

—C. G. Jung

and consciousness we share with all life forms on the planet, we must each gather up the fragments of our own shattered and distorted reflections within the calm center of our spiritual eye. But discovering the truth about ourselves requires willingness and committed effort. Most of us act and react from deeply embedded patterns in the brain, patterns created by memories of habitual, insensible ways of being and seeing. Through a visionary experience of wholeness, it is possible to see beyond these patterns, transcend a distorted world view, and perceive the "sacred hoop" we share with all people, life forms, and with our Mother—the Earth.

The mandala is a potent tool for this mystical, visionary process of reintegration and healing. It helps us gain access to enigmatic states of consciousness in which our thoughts can be realigned and our creative imaginations infused with a deep spiritual purpose: to reflect the harmonics of the divine and the beauty of the holy universal connections. This chapter presents you with meditations and a drawing exercise to help you address and restore to health your own connections to the divine whole as expressed in your relationships with nature, the

The fact that images (mandalas) of this kind have under certain circumstances a considerable therapeutic effect on their authors is empirically proved and also readily understandable, in that they often represent very bold attempts to see and put together apparently irreconcilable opposites and bridge over apparently hopeless splits. Even the mere attempt in this direction usually has a healing effect . . . [2]

—C. G. Jung

FIG. 5.1. EXPLORING NEW PATTERNS OF BELONGING.

There are ways to become part of a mandala in order to explore new patterns of belonging and wholeness. Marion Weber, at Commonweal Cancer Program, Bolinas, California, has developed a powerful tool, *The Group Sandtray,* which enables eight people to uncover the innate wholeness in themselves and their relationships. Marion described the process:

People have the opportunity to pass through a room of symbolic toys and objects, pick those which have personal appeal and then sit at a round, sand-filled table and place their objects in the sand in whatever way feels right to them. In the spirit of unknowing, one at a time, each person tells the group the story of the scene they have created in the sand.

It is an experience in trusting our deepest intuition. As we share our personal unconscious wisdom, more and more of the collective wisdom emerges. We witness this process and become aware of our participation in it, often for the first time. By the close of this experience we realize that something sacred has been created through us by our willingness to surrender to the mystery. It is a healing for everyone.

Marion Weber

Earth, and other human beings. The symbols you receive as you perform the meditations will be illumined and activated by love, light, and sacred sound, and will have the power to override the negative images stored in our brains by reflecting our sacred interconnections with all beings. The mandala you create will reveal the interconnections between the images you receive.

Making a Sacred Connection With Nature

East Indian, Tibetan, and most indigenous cultures perceive all life forms as sacred—a part of divine manifestation. Animals, birds, flowers, trees, humans, and all other life forms arise from the womb of the Earth. Interconnected, they form a symphony of nature that feeds and nurtures us on our spiritual journey. Like St. Francis of Assisi, Aztec Mazatl Galindo finds speaking with the Earth and animals a perfectly natural process of attunement:

Anne Herrick

In traditional languages such as Aztec or Mayan or Quechua, you can speak with the elements because they are alive. And we all know we are part of those elements. We are Fire. We are Earth. We are Water . . . In these languages you talk with the Earth, you talk with the birds and animals with their same voice, with the same heart . . . There is nothing strange about this because we are part of the same creation. And if the creation is part of everything around, below, and above you, then by communicating you are extending yourself and expanding yourself to the point where you actually become the eagle, the jaguar, the flower, the roots, the tree. You don't separate yourself as a human and merely intellectualize your connection and relationship to the rest of creation.[3]

In my workshops, I help people reestablish this sacred relationship with birds, animals, and the Earth by using shamanic journeys to the underworld, meditative methods of yoga, or combinations of both. Both processes consist of an inward journey to the world of spiritual realities. Tibetan Buddhist practice, for example, integrates elements of yoga with Bon shamanism in its meditations and art, using these elements in a highly transformed way to further one's progress toward enlightenment.

A number of shamanic traditions use steady drum beats to alter the consciousness of the person traveling to the underworld to meet empowering animal spirits. This book is not intended to teach shamanic practice. But if you are practiced in this way of journeying, you can use it instead of the following meditation—or perhaps vary the methods you use—to gain access to the spiritual realms of nature.

Setting a Clear Intention for the Inner Journey

Before beginning the meditation, clarify your intention to make a sacred and healing connection with the Earth and with those spiritual energies of birds or animals that can best empower you. It is important to remain humble, open, and receptive to what is revealed to you. Even if you have a favorite animal or bird, it may not show up in revelation. The Divine manifests for us both in ways our psyches can understand and in ways in which they need help. For example, you might be shown an animal you fear, just so you can make peace with its energies in order to acquire the power to overcome your fear. Or, you might be shown animals you never thought much about but whose strength or attributes you need to develop—the eagle's keen vision, for example, or its ability to fly high and see a greater perspective on the world. It is

Beth Susanne

important that you trust the process to reveal the special meanings that the birds or animals have for you.

As an example, for many years I was very fearful of snakes. Often in my dreams I saw powerful cobras radiating menacing, green incandescent light. The cobra imagery I received in my dreams represented for me the transformative *Kundalini,* or serpent power, as it is called in India. *Kundalini* is the potent creative energy of Shakti, coiled at the base of the spine. With special yoga practice, this energy rises up through the central spine into the brain to create a psycho-physical transformation. Since *Kundalini* is a creative force that resides within, I realized that it could be used constructively or destructively, depending on my state of consciousness. As I became accustomed to the sight of the cobras in my dreams and lost my fear of them, I overcame my fears of my own creative powers and made peace with their energy. In the process, a strange thing began to happen in the outer world. I began to encounter all kinds of nonpoisonous snakes lying in the middle of my path. These unexpected sightings tested my resolve to overcome my fear. I found that if I gathered my courage and remained fearless, I could greet them with love. Then the snakes would remain still and I could step over them, trusting that they would do me no harm.

The saints and sages who could converse with animals did so in a divine meditative state of consciousness in which their magnetic spiritual vibrations could calm and tame even the most ferocious of beasts. From the perspective of Eastern spiritual philosophy, the process you are about to undertake is really about taming and healing the wild energies within yourself in order to achieve a calm, empowered, and expanded level of realization—and a love for all life.

Materials

Use the same materials, black paper and colored pencils, as listed in Chapter 4, p. 82.

Meditation: *Blessing the Materials*

Before you begin bless the materials as you did in Chapter 2, p. 41.

Key Points to Remember: *Meditating on Natural Symbols*

◆ Create a sacred workspace surrounded and protected by Divine Light.

◆ Before you begin, ask with clear intention to have those spiritual energies of animals or birds revealed that will help you heal your connection with nature.

◆ Meditate on filling your body with Divine Light, keeping your attention focused in the third eye while meditating.

◆ Relax and allow the spiritual images to arise spontaneously. Humbly accept what is revealed.

◆ Infuse the image or images with unconditional love.

◆ Further activate your sacred relationship by chanting *Aum* out loud three times.

MEDITATION: *Journey into the Divine Realities of Nature*

Prepare a sacred space by visualizing yourself surrounded in white light. If it helps, set up a ritual altar with a burning candle and flowers. Rituals help change consciousness by directing the mind to the inner meditative state.

Relax, sit in a meditative pose, and slowly take three deep breaths. On each exhalation, release all tension and negative thoughts from your mind and body. Gently quiet your breathing.

❖

Keeping your heart receptive, close your eyes, and gently focus your attention between the eyebrows at the center called the spiritual eye. In the spiritual eye, imagine pure white light radiantly present and full of blessings for and within you.

❖

Meditate on the blessing energy. Direct it down through your neck and into your heart, feeling warmth and love. Continue directing it to all the organs, cells, and atoms in your body. Imagine the light in your body increasing and becoming incandescent.

❖

Bring your attention back to the third eye and imagine yourself soaring like a bird high above the Earth. Now imagine that the Earth is within your heart. Open your heart to embrace the sacred energies of the Earth with love. Stay with this part of the meditation until you *feel* a heart connection, an attunement with the Earth.

❖

Still focusing in the third eye, humbly ask with clear intention to receive the perfect animal or bird images that will help you heal your connection with nature. Relax and wait in meditative silence for their forms to appear spontaneously.

❖

After receiving the spiritual essence of animals or birds, humbly give thanks.

❖

Next, bring the image of that spiritual essence into your heart and infuse it with unconditional love.

❖

In your heart, focus on the animal or bird's luminous spiritual quality, and activate your relationship by chanting three times the sacred sound of *Aum*.

❖

Stay a while in the meditative state, allowing the light and sound vibrations to spread through your body/mind.

❖

When you are ready, gently come back from the meditative state and in silence begin to make some small sketches in your journal or notebook. Then proceed to drawing your mandala.

❖

Barbara Rifkin

Exercise 1: *Symbolic Drawing of Birds and Animals*

The following exercise is designed to help you to embrace the divine interconnectedness we share with the spiritual energies of animals and birds by merging meditation and mandala drawing. After establishing this sacred connection through meditation, symbolize the spirit of the animals and birds in a simple manner using combined geometric shapes of rectangles, circles, ovals, and squares as in some of the examples in this chapter. Sometimes people get two or more images from the meditative process. If this happens to you, you can combine images of all of them within one mandala in a dynamic way.

1. First, using the white pencil, create a circle on the black page. Then create a line drawing of the imagery you receive in the meditation inside the circle (see Fig. 5.2).

2. Don't worry if you see an animal or bird you think you cannot draw. If you are actually inhibited by a fear of drawing, trace the outline of a bird or animal that you find in a book or magazine. You can then enlarge or reduce the tracing on a photocopy machine. Don't try to copy a photograph or image realistically on your own, however, unless you have had a lot of training in that direction.

3. After you have completed the line drawing, put all references away and begin radiating it using the white pencil.

4. After you have finished with the white pencil, go into meditation, holding the image in your third eye, and ask for the colors of the animals and birds to be revealed to you.

5. Then use all the rainbow colors—coloring freely and spontaneously from your imagination. This is important, because unless you let your own imagination guide your pencil rather than trying to copy a photograph or someone else's rendering of wildlife, you will be unable to understand the spiritual essence of the animals or to transcend any creative fears you have of symbolic drawing.

6. Whenever you run into a creative block, meditate again and ask for guidance from the animals or birds of your vision. Become one with the animal or bird; do not remain intellectually aloof. Feel what it is like to be in that animal or bird body and to see and experience from that spiritual perspective. In the yogic and shamanic traditions, you expand consciousness to the point where you actually become one with the animal or bird you are shown in the inner vision. That way, you do not separate yourself as a human and merely intellectualize your connection and relationship.

Sylvia Nachlinger

A human being is a part of the whole called by us "the universe," a part limited in time and space. He experiences himself, his thoughts and feelings, as something separate from the rest—a kind of optical delusion of his consciousness. This delusion is a kind of prison for us, restricting us to our personal desires and affection for a few persons nearest to us. Our task must be to free ourselves from this prison by widening our circle of understanding and compassion to embrace all living creatures and the whole of nature in its beauty.[4]

—Albert Einstein

Forgiveness is one of the greatest gifts of spiritual life. It enables us to be released from the sorrows of the past . . . Forgiveness is simply an act of the heart, a movement to let go of the pain, the resentment, the outrage that you have carried as a burden for so long. It is an easing of your own heart and an acknowledgment that, no matter how strongly you may condemn and have suffered from the evil deeds of another, you will not put another human being out of your heart. We have all been harmed, just as we have all at times harmed ourselves and others.[5]

—Jack Kornfield

Key Points to Remember: *Creating a Dynamic Drawing*

◆ Bless the art materials before you begin drawing the mandala.

◆ While drawing, become one with the animal or bird. Feel its energy flow through your body and your heart.

◆ Remember, you are capturing the spiritual essence in symbolic form. It is not important that you do a physically realistic rendering of a bird or animal.

◆ If you are truly afraid of drawing, trace an outline of a bird or animal.

◆ Dynamically exaggerate the size of the image to enhance its power and energy.

◆ While drawing, continue to ask for inner guidance from the animal or bird of your vision.

◆ Radiate the drawing with the scale of white first, deciding what you will leave black.

◆ Then meditate again, asking for the rainbow luster of the animals to be revealed. Allow yourself to color freely from imagination and inner guidance.

Opening Your Heart to Inclusive Love

Making a mandala for someone with whom we have difficulties can be a potent form of healing psychological and spiritual wounds. By symbolically reflecting the soul's nature—the spiritual equality we share with all human beings—we can overcome cultural bias and religious prejudices and transcend gender differences and issues. Each soul is a spark of the divine, completely unique, with the potential to be original in its expression of divinity. As proof of this, I have used the "Expanding the Light" exercise in the first chapter with large groups of people and have found that every person's image, pattern of light, or way of expressing light is unique. All the mandalas in this book were created by different people. Not one mandala is the same, and yet each is remarkably beautiful.

Instead of honoring and fostering this creative uniqueness and the expression of the One Light we share, we usually *exclude* most of the human race from our hearts and minds because their skin color, education, culture, religion, or sex is different from ours. Our eyes are blind to and our hearts contracted against the beauty of diversity, and yet we react with hurt if, on the basis of *our* differences, others exclude us, cause us harm, or reject our points of view. Wars have been fought over differences.

Without a transcendental nondual perspective, religious or human relationships across these differences are all but impossible. It has been the saints and sages in all the spiritual traditions who have traversed the illusory boundaries and gloried in our spiritual nature and the unity we all share. Though procreation as we understand it involves physical differences between the genders, the soul is a spiritual essence and is neither male nor female. Our bodies are merely vehicles, holy temples in which our souls manifest their divinity.

Regaining a Soul Perspective

We in the West have lost touch with the knowledge of our souls and our shared divinity, and at times we injure each other out of ignorance. But through mystical communion with the Divine, we can see past our differences, forgive those who have injured us, and mend the hurt we have caused others. As Yogananda says:

In the consciousness of one who is immersed in the divine love of God, there is no deception, no narrowness of caste or creed, no boundaries of any kind. When you experience that divine love, you will see no difference between flower and beast, between one human being and another. You will commune with all nature, and you will love equally all mankind. [6]

To heal our damaged human relationships, it is necessary that we let go of the fear that keeps us in an ego state. It is also important to

FIG. 5.2.

These computer-generated drawings illustrate the key points to creating a dynamic drawing.

Joan Malcolm

Traditionally, in ancient times there were different sacred sites as well as actual buildings in which universal wisdom was shared . . . these were places . . . in which your spirit would bloom as a flower, as an extension of the creator, as an expression of this creativity. This was a place where you learned not only the beauty of art, but the profound effect art can have in your mind, your psyche, your spirit, and your surroundings. And this was applied on a daily basis as a blessing and in service to the community . . .

This unity between art, science, and spirituality is central to all native cultures . . . Also important is the concept of the circle and the square as geometrical forms used as the foundation for our ancient cities. Our people made these buildings not just because they look nice or for grandiose reasons. They have a sense of purpose. They are sacred places.[7]

—Mazatl Galindo

acknowledge and release any feelings of hated, anger, jealousy, lust, or wishes for another person's harm. Many people come to my workshops and retreats with a need to heal deep psychological and spiritual wounds. Many have suffered incest and other sexual abuse, spiritual crises, and unresolved family conflicts. They may be undergoing psychotherapy to relieve their problems. But many find that using meditation and the mandala process to change their consciousness is a nonjudgmental, loving, and supportive way to begin ridding the body/mind of its soul-ignorance through forgiveness and to experience states of bliss and unconditional love.

Love Beyond Emotions

All of us want love and acceptance, but true unconditional love is beyond emotions—beyond actions and reactions, anger and blame. True love is peace, bliss, understanding, and the acknowledgment of the divinity in all. However, it takes practice to love unconditionally. Our close relationships are a place to begin. After healing, we can expand our consciousness until we are lovingly embracing *all* people as our brothers and sisters bound by one humanity. This is the love of Mother Teresa, Gandhi, Christ, and the Buddha. Each of them understood that the soul is perfect, and knew how to see through dark emotions and negative thought into the soul's light.

Patricia Andersson

MEDITATION: *Healing Through Soul Perception*

Before beginning the meditation, identify clearly in your mind a relationship you would like to heal. Choose a relationship that has been troubled; it might even be with a person who has died. Though you will meditate with the intention to heal, try to rid yourself of all expectations as to the outcome of this process. You are taking responsibility for your own healing and attempting to perceive the light of another's soul. Whether or not the other person responds in a more positive way to you after the meditation is not the point. You need only unconditionally engage your whole heart, mind, and soul to receive the divine healing blessings that, without doubt, will flow to you.

Create a sacred workspace surrounded and protected by Divine Light.

❖

Become clear and committed to one relationship you would like to heal.

❖

With your attention focused in the third eye, hold an image of that person.

❖

Let go of fear, and try to imagine the person's physical appearance in a neutral way, leaving behind, as much as possible, the emotional feelings he or she evokes.

❖

In the spiritual eye, see the essence of the person's soul and picture it as divinely radiant light. With your heart open, send a ray of unconditional love to that soul.

❖

Ask with clear intention in meditation that the perfect spiritual symbol for helping to heal that relationship be revealed to you.

❖

Relax and allow the symbol to arise spontaneously. Humbly accept what is revealed.

❖

Bring the symbol into your heart and infuse it with unconditional love.

❖

Further activate this healing image by chanting *Aum* three times. Then proceed with the following exercise.

❖

Materials

Use the same materials, black paper and colored pencils, as listed in Chapter 4, p. 82.

Meditation: *Blessing the Materials*

Before you begin bless the materials as you did in Chapter 2, p. 41.

Female and male Navajo sandpainting images

Exercise 2: *Creating a Mandala to Heal a Relationship*

After the meditation, unconditionally engage your whole heart, mind, and soul in the process of creating a mandala.

1. Using the white pencil, create a circle on the black page. Then create a line drawing of the symbol you receive in the meditation.

2. Radiate the line drawing with white pencil and decide what areas you will leave black. (If you feel uncertain about what to do, review Chapter 3, Constructing a Mandala, p. 62.)

3. After the white color is complete, go back into meditation, holding the image in your third eye, and ask for the perfect colors of this symbol to be revealed to you.

4. Bring the colored symbol into your heart and activate it by chanting *Aum* three times.

5. Then, with strong will and intention, pour all the love of your heart into the coloring process and ask for guidance anytime you feel fear.

6. When you finish, if it feels appropriate, give the person your completed mandala as a gift of unconditional love. But have no expectations as to the outcome of the process.

Native American motif

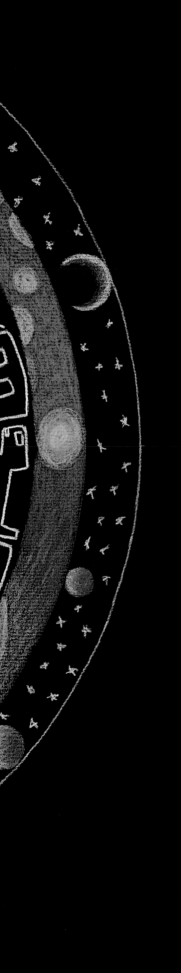

Nature is beautiful and kind,

She is always on my mind.

But I'm afraid she's getting ill,

She's suffering an oil spill.

Her ozone layer comes to mind;

It's getting very hard to find.

She's got a fever (global warming),

She's getting hotter every morning.

She has congestion, acid rain,

She says she has an ocean pain.

She has pollution, nonbiodegradables;

Her trees have been made into chairs and tables.

Her rain forest lungs are getting smaller,

And smoke stacks yet are being built taller.

She's sick and if something's not done fast,

Mother Nature may not last.

—Eric Hogle, age 10

Jennifer Scott

By symbolically reflecting the soul's nature—the spiritual equality we share with all human beings—we can overcome cultural bias and religious prejudices and transcend physical gender differences and issues. Each soul is a spark of the Divine, is completely unique, and has the latent potential to be original in its expression of divinity.

Summary

You can do the meditations in this chapter any number of times to help in revising consciousness. In conjunction with this process, as you become imbued with an understanding of spiritual interconnections, try to embrace more of the beauty and wonder of nature. Speak to the animals, flowers, and birds; tell them you love them and the luminous qualities of their innocent souls. For most people, it is far easier to relate lovingly to animals, flowers, and birds than to humans. In India, people greet one another with the salutation *namaste.* It means "the highest in me greets and acknowledges the highest in you." If done with deep concentration and devotion, this salutation honors the other person as an already enlightened being. In our culture people might think you strange if you said this to them, but in the silence of your heart and mind, you can acknowledge enlightenment and imagine beyond all difficulties, conceiving the people you meet and work with every day as already fully enlightened. As all of us take responsibility for transforming our own vision and for developing our creative gifts from an illumined perspective, we add to the beauty and harmony around us.

Notes

[1] Richard Wilhelm, trans., *The Secret of the Golden Flower, with a Foreword and Commentary by C. G. Jung* (New York and London: Harcourt Brace Jovanovich, 1962), 102.

[2] C. G. Jung, *Mandala Symbolism,* Bollingen Series (Princeton: Princeton University Press, 1973), 5.

[3] Mazatl Galindo, "The Flowering Earth: Ancient Wisdom in Mexico," *Noetic Sciences Review* (Summer 1993), 29, 30.

[4] Albert Einstein, quoted by Jack Kornfield in *A Path With Heart* (New York: Bantam Books, 1993), 288.

[5] Jack Kornfield, *A Path With Heart,* 284-85.

[6] Paramahansa Yogananda, *Where There Is Light* (Los Angeles: Self-Realization Fellowship, 1988), 133.

[7] Galindo, "Flowering," 30.

Jessica Shapley

CHAPTER 6:

ILLUMINATING SACRED AND MYSTICAL REALITIES

You are the artist, you are the raw material, you are the work of art and you are the reality behind the work of art . . . One experiences ecstasy when one discovers the creator in one, as oneself.

The whole of life is a process whereby the unmanifest becomes manifest. Divine Creativity is completed by human creativity. Of all the qualities in your being, the one that is most God-like is creativity.

—Pir Vilayat Inayat Khan

Just as the creation of God, that is, humankind, never ceases to come to an end, but rather, continually develops, so also the works of humankind shall not disappear. Those things that tend toward God shall shine forth in the heavens, while those that are devilish shall become notorious through their ill effects.

—Hildegard of Bingen

THE MEDITATION EXERCISES IN THIS CHAPTER FOCUS on ways to deepen the relationship of your soul with the universal Light of Consciousness. By awakening to the fullness of who we really are, we express the deeper transpersonal and mystical realities of the soul. The greatest saints and sages were ecstatic, fully illumined artist/scientists and healers whose greatest work was their own self-realization. Each was a unique expression of spiritual genius. Saint Hildegard of Bingen, an eleventh-century Benedictine abbess, is a moving and enduring example. She was one of the greatest mystic prophets and female spiritual geniuses of the Western Christian tradition.

Saint Hildegard and the Mandala

Hildegard was a theologian, musician, poet, dramatist, scientist, and physician. She also was a leader of men and women in creation centered spirituality, a unique integration of intellect and spiritual intuition. From the time she was very young Hildegard had spiritual visions. Later in life, when she was an abbess, her fear of expressing these visions made her ill. She was not cured until she had the courage to record, with the help of scribes, her sacred visions in words and painted mandalas. Like all great saints, Hildegard was a humble channel through which the Divine could flow. She was guided by God to "transmit for the benefit of humanity an accurate account of *what you see with your inner eye*, and what you hear with the *inner ear* of your soul." (italics mine) Her visionary focus on inner light and sounds in order to reach and transcribe spiritual realities parallels Tibetan and Hindu yogic spiritual practices. After one of her visions, she wrote:

> *I—wretched and fragile creature that I am—began then to write with a trembling hand, even though I was shaken by countless illnesses . . . While I set about my task of writing, I looked up again to the true and living light as to what I should write down . . . I saw it with the inner eye of my spirit and grasped it with my inner ear. In this connection I was never in a condition similar to sleep, nor was I ever in a state of spiritual rapture, as I have already emphasized in connection with my earlier visions. In addition, I did not explain anything in testimony of the truth that I might have derived from the realm of human sentiments, but rather only what I have received from the heavenly mysteries.[1]*

Saint Hildegard was not schooled, as the Tibetan monks are, in an orthodox tradition of mandala making. But her unorthodox use of the mandala demonstrates even more clearly than traditional practices its potential for expressing spiritual truth. Her mandalic imagery arose naturally out of her sense of wholeness, and the sacred circle was a perfect vehicle for illuminating revelations from God. Out of the visual and aural evidence she received of God's presence, Hildegard made art from the iconography of Catholicism that resonated with the universal light of truth.

Hildegard's creation centered spirituality was rooted in her perception that "humankind, full of all creative possibilities, is God's work. Humankind alone is called to assist God. Humankind is called to co-create." Her focus closely echoes the Hindu Vedic teachings as expressed by Yogananda:

> *The divine purpose of creation, so far as man's reason can grasp it, is expounded in the Vedas. The rishis taught that each human being has been created by God as a soul that will uniquely manifest some special attribute of the Infinite before resuming its Absolute Identity.[2]*

Like Hildegard, we are unique sparks of divinity meant to reveal an essence of God that is uniquely ours to express. In order to become a channel for divine revelation—that is, to become an illumined mystic/artist—it is important to rededicate oneself to God and selfless service. It is helpful to set aside some time each day for deep medita-

The human person is the form and the fullness of creation. In humankind, God brings to fullness all his creation. God created humankind, so that humankind might cultivate the earthly and thereby create the heavenly. Humankind should be the banner of divinity. Divinity is aimed at humanity.[3]

—**Hildegard of Bingen**

tion that is wedded to the deep desire to awaken and heal from soul-ignorance and express the truth of one's soul-nature. In order to change our world, we have to change ourselves. This means becoming fully empowered to allow the harmonious inner truth and light of our souls to shine forth. But because many religious traditions are, like science, locked into dogma and rational thinking, the creative aspect of soul expression has been suppressed, calling forth in us the deepest longings for fulfillment.

From Procreation to Cocreation

To use your creative energies to help your soul evolve, it is important to understand the original intention of sacred art: it is a meditative science of yoga designed to channel creative energies toward the radiant awakening of spiritual genius. This transformative process redirects outward-flowing procreative sexual energies and centers them within the spinal channel so that they rise up through the chakras to the spiritual centers in the brain to be used cocreatively. At certain stages of spiritual development, celibacy is recommended because of the tremendous energy and discipline needed to complete the alchemy of enlightenment. This is the essential purpose of the practice of *Raja, Kundalini,* and *Kriya* yoga.

In the Hindu tradition, as this potent creative energy moves up from its source at the base of the spine, it transforms the body and mind into an increasingly subtle body of light. This transformation prepares the body/mind to contain the superconscious light of Christ

---

FIG. 6.1. *Hildegard of Bingen's Second Vision: On the Construction of the World.* LATINUM CODEX, 1942, BIBLIOTECA STATALE, LUCCA, ITALY. REPRODUCED BY PERMISSION OF SCALA/ART RESOURCE, N.Y.

In this vision, God reveals to Hildegard that humanity is gifted with divinity and that the world is whole and ceaselessly expressing the creative love of God. God says:

> For the shape of the world exists everlastingly in the knowledge of the true Love which is God: constantly circling, wonderful for human nature, and such that it is not consumed by age and cannot be increased by anything new . . . in its workings the Godhead is like a wheel, a whole. In no way is it to be divided because the Godhead has neither beginning nor end.[4]

FIG. 6.2. *Hildegard of Bingen's Third Vision: On Human Nature* (right).

Hildegard's knowledge of medicine comes through God's revelation, in which she is shown the nature of the soul and cause of human illness. This revelation, similar to the Eastern teachings and practice of Raja Yoga, is about the integration of body and soul through breath and mind control to increase the life force within the body. As Hildegard says:

> *. . . longing affects the human heart. If we humans, whose natural quality corresponds to that cosmic complaint, draw into ourselves and expel again air transformed in this way so that our soul can receive it in order to bring it farther within our body, the humors in our organism will also be changed and will bring to our body . . . either illness or good health. This occurs when we, whose goodwill is in agreement with that breath, give up our longing for evil and oppose it.[5]*

FIG. 6.3. *Hildegard of Bingen's Fourth Vision: On the Articulation of the Body* (facing page).

In this vision God reveals to Hildegard the meaning of the Word (*Aum, Amen*) as a way of manifesting and mirroring God's divinity through forms constructed of light and sound. She said that the line from the Gospel of John, "In the beginning was the Word," is to be understood in the following way:

> *I am the day that does not shine by the sun; rather by me the sun is ignited. I am the Reason that is not made perceptible by anyone else; rather, I am the One by whom every reasonable being draws breath. And so to gaze at my countenance I have created mirrors in which I consider all the wonders of my originality, which will never cease. I have prepared for myself these mirror forms so that they may resonate in a song of praise. For I have a voice like the thunderbolt by which I keep in motion the entire universe in the living sounds of all creation . . . By my Word, which was and is without beginning in myself, I caused a mighty light to emerge.[6]*

or the Buddha. As an analogy, you might imagine that most of us possess the creative energy of a sixty-watt light bulb while our actual potential is to wield a voltage a million times more powerful. Without the wisdom and the creative enlightenment of the Great Ones, we use this sixty-watt mentality to unleash the energies of the atom. We are divine children playing with fire.

Creativity: *A Spiritual Evolutionary Power*

As I continue to take this work out into the world, I have become increasingly aware of the limited way in which most people regard the function of creativity. This seems to be especially true for women, who have access to very few spiritual role models. Perhaps owing in part to the influence of our mechanistically-based science, creativity is one of the least understood and least developed capacities within our society. Most people associate it with egocentricity, eccentricity, instability, and even insanity. Creativity has been viewed as the prerogative or anomaly of a few, rather than as a divine gift and potential within all souls. Our

present view of the artist needs to expand from a narrow definition of "one who paints or sculpts" to "one who is in the process of Self-realization."

This expanded definition of creativity makes it a function in *all* people and a process that unfolds throughout all fields of endeavor. Someday the material sciences themselves will be seen as creative and subjective rather than exclusively rational and objective. In the future, medicine will understand the nature and function of consciousness and creativity as it relates to health and healing, and art as it is known today will merge with science. The computer is already contributing to this integration. It reveals visually the underlying beauty and ever-changing radiant patterns

Buffy Hart

of fractals and other complex mathematical formulas that demonstrate a nonlinear, ongoing, creative process.

The following meditation focuses on redirecting your consciousness to facilitate the upward flow of creative energy into the spinal column, permitting you to open yourself to higher states of creativity based on love and wisdom. In the following meditation, you will intone the sacred Hindu Sanskrit sounds for each of the six chakras. You will start with the lowest chakra at the base of the spine and work up to the spiritual eye. Notice that in most pictures of saints the eyes are uplifted in a state of ecstasy. Energy follows thought or consciousness. In saints, consciousness and creative energy are focused in the third eye, the eye of spiritual vision.

So it is with our thoughts and inner energies. If we concentrate our consciousness on procreative thoughts, our creative energies are drawn to the genitals near the region of the second chakra. If we are focused on compassion and loving unconditionally, our consciousness and creative energies flow upward into the heart, the psychoenergetic area known as the heart chakra. Sri Ramakrishna, one of the greatest spiritual geniuses of the last century, describes his experience of chakras and the focus of consciousness from a Vedanta perspective. He says:

> The Vedanta speaks of seven planes in which the mind moves and works. The ordinary man's mind moves and works only in the three lower centers and is content with satisfying itself through the common appetites: eating, drinking, sleeping, and begetting. But when it reaches the fourth center opposite the heart, man sees a divine effulgence. From this state, however, he often lapses back to the three lower centers. When the mind comes to the fifth center opposite the throat the spiritual aspirant cannot speak of anything but God . . . Even from this state a man may slip down; he should therefore be very watchful. But he need not have any fear of a fall when the mind reaches the sixth center, level with the junction of the eyebrows. He gets the vision of the 'Paramatman' (Oversoul) and remains always in 'Samadhi.'[7]

In order to awaken latent spiritual genius, it is necessary to open the heart to create from an imaginal consciousness of unconditional love, wisdom, and spiritual inspiration through the light of the inner eye. The meditation described here is meant to focus your most profound creative energy in order to pour it, in all its illuminating power, into a mandala. Having gradually approached this final exercise through the lessons in the preceding chapters, you have prepared and practiced gaining access to your own light and merging with the One by means of the mandalic circle.

The light is neither inside nor outside the self. Mountains, rivers, sun, moon, and the whole earth are all this light, so it is not only in the self. All the operations of intelligence, knowledge, and wisdom are also this light, so it is not outside the self. The light of heaven and earth fills the universe; the light of one individual also naturally extends through the heavens and covers the earth. Therefore once you turn the light around, everything in the world is turned around.

The light rays are concentrated upward into the eyes; this is the great key of the human body. You should reflect on this. If you do not sit quietly each day, this light flows and whirls, stopping who knows where. If you can sit quietly for a while, all time—ten thousand ages, a thousand lifetimes—is penetrated from this. All phenomena revert to stillness. Truly inconceivable is this sublime truth.[8]

—The Secret of the Golden Flower

Intoning Sacred Sounds of the Chakras

For thousands of years, sacred sounds (mantras) have been used by yogis to harmonize the body/mind. Intoning the sacred sounds of the chakras helps expand and harmonize consciousness into divine oneness with the universal and spiritually inclusive sound of *Aum*. Each chakra has a specific sound. You will intone each three times, starting at the base of the spine and progressing until you intone the sacred sound of *Aum* in the sixth chakra or spiritual eye. By the time you have chanted all the sounds in succession, you will be able to experience your whole body/mind as it resonates with these sacred vibrations.

Before you begin, prepare a sacred space by visualizing yourself surrounded in white light. Then study the accompanying chart, which shows the order and name of the sacred sounds of each of the chakra centers. The English transliteration of *A* is pronounced *àh*.

Sanskrit Sound Locations

AUM	The center between the eyebrows
HAM	Throat center
YAM	Heart center
RAM	Navel center
VAM	Below the navel
LAM	Base of the spine

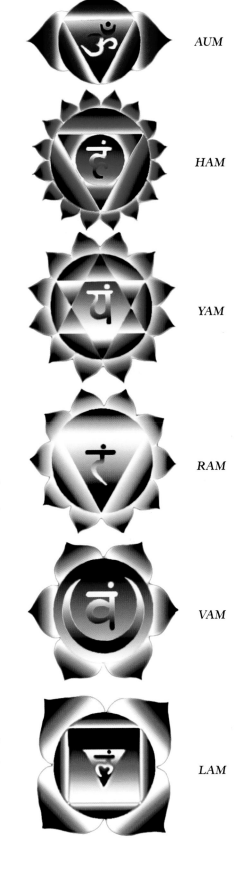

AUM

HAM

YAM

RAM

VAM

LAM

FIG. 6.4. A YOGI RADIATING LIGHT AND SOUND. COMPUTER-GENERATED BY AUTHOR.

When intoning the Sanskrit sounds of the chakras, the body/mind will resonate beautiful, luminous sound wave patterns. This computer-enhanced image gives an intuitive glimpse of the effect that sacred sound has on the body/mind. The image is also meant to convey the human body as a sacred temple for the unfolding Kundalini energy moving from the base of the spine to the top of the head. As Sri Shankaranarayanan, says:

> *In the human body, the place of the Bindu (lingam, the static male principle) is at the top of the spinal column in the thousand-petalled lotus center in the head. The Trikona (triangle) is at the bottom of the spinal column in the Muladhara, the base-center. The Divine Mother is the coiled energy Kundalini who traverses up and down the path between the two centers in her courses of evolution and involution ... The whole creation is the outcome of the union of* linga *and* yoni, *the Bindu and the Trikona.*[9]

Materials

Use the same materials, black paper and colored pencils, as listed in Chapter 4, p. 82.

Meditation: *Blessing the Materials*

Before you begin, bless the materials as you did in Chapter 2, p. 41.

MEDITATION: *Revelation Through Sacred Sound*

Relax, sit in a meditative pose, and slowly take three deep breaths. On each exhalation, release all tension and negative thoughts from your mind and body. Gently quiet your breathing.

❖

Close your eyes and gently focus your attention at the base of the spine. Repeat slowly and with devotion the sacred sound of LAM three times: *La-a-am, La-a-am, La-a-am.* Be conscious of how this sound resonates in this center.

❖

Next, concentrate your attention in the space between the base of the spine and the navel. Intone VAM three times: *Va-a-am, Va-a-am, Va-a-am.*

❖

Put your conscious attention at the navel and intone RAM three times: *Ra-a-am, Ra-a-am, Ra-a-am.*

❖

Next, in your heart center, while remaining open and receptive, intone the sacred sound YAM three time: *Ya-a-am, Ya-a-am, Ya-a-am.*

❖

Bring your focus to the throat center and intone the sound HAM: *Ha-a-am, Ha-a-am, Ha-a-am.*

❖

Now, in the spiritual eye, intone AUM (OM) three times: *O-o-o—m-m-m, Oo-o—m-m-m, O-o-o—m-m-m.*

❖

While your body/mind is experiencing this sacred resonance, keep the attention at the spiritual center.

❖

Ask with humble receptivity to have revealed to you the perfect symbol for expressing your soul's nature—a symbol that can lead you to a deeper relationship with the divine within you.

❖

After receiving the symbol humbly, give thanks and bring that image into your heart and infuse it with unconditional love.

❖

Activate the symbol by chanting three times out loud the sacred sound of AUM while seeing the symbol radiant and glowing within your heart.

❖

Stay in the meditative state for a while, allowing the light and sound vibrations to spread through your body/mind.

❖

When you are ready, gently come back from the meditative state and in silence begin drawing your mandala.

❖

Exercise: *Expressing Your Soul's Divinity*

1. Draw a white circle on black paper and then draw the outline of the symbol you received in meditation. Anytime you are afraid, chant with devotion the sacred sounds of the chakras. The symbol may be repeated more than once and may be exaggerated in size to fill the whole of the circle.

2. Remember that you are raising your creative energies so that you become an inspired cocreative channel for the soul's love and light to flow through. Remain open and receptive and let the drawing draw you.

3. When you have completed the line drawing, illuminate it in white. Concentrate on making it as radiant and alive as you can by pouring all the love of your heart into the process.

4. Then, go back into meditation, holding the symbol in your third eye while chanting the sacred sounds of the chakras in the same order as before.

5. When you have intoned the *Aum* sound, ask with intention to have revealed the perfect colors for this symbol. Then color the mandala.

6. The soul reflects through the mandala its rainbow essence and unity in white light. Spontaneously and joyfully mirror your soul's knowledge and wisdom through the colorful mandalic patterns of light and sound.

7. Hang up the mandala several times during the drawing process to get some perspective—to see if you are bringing enough light into the drawing.

8. When you have completed the process, once again hang it on the wall. Over several days, weeks, or even months, you may find that new revelations will come from this symbol. People often tell me that they understood the meaning of their symbol only after living with it for a while.

Roda Patel, M.D.

Kay Brockway

FIG 6.5. KAY BROCKWAY'S MANDALA DRAWING.

Many seekers on a spiritual quest ask: "Who am I?" Kay's mystical drawing reflects an essence of who she really is. She says:

Drawing this mandala was just like the process of falling in love—which is exactly how it affected me. The question I asked, as I sat down to the blank paper was "Who Am I?" Suddenly this beautiful, divine image appeared in my mind's eye, that radiated infinite love and compassion—a face so sweet—serene yet filled with life and beauty. As I worked on this drawing a continual flow of energy poured out from it, to my heart and body—wave currents of bliss rising and falling. It was as though the answer to my question came with every movement of the pencils. I was almost sorry when it was finished, but the feeling returns when I look into those eyes.

Materials

On the day you visit the labyrinth (see next page), take a small drawing pad or journal with you to record the symbol and any words you receive in the center of the labyrinth. Afterward, find a quiet place near the labyrinth, or go home to draw your mandala using the same materials, black paper and colored pencils, as listed in Chapter 4, p. 82.

MEDITATION: *Pilgrimage of the Mystic Soul*

Here are Dr. Artress's suggestions for walking the labyrinth. To blend mandala drawing with labyrinth walking, I have included meditative suggestions in brackets.

First, walk the labyrinth three times so you feel comfortable with it as a meditation tool. [The labyrinth is not a maze; you will not get lost.]

❖

There are three stages to walking the labyrinth As you step on the path, you enter the first stage, purgation. *When walking the path, think of it as a process of letting go, emptying out, releasing, or shedding, so that your mind becomes a receptive empty container.* [As you enter the path, quiet your mind, and visualize yourself shedding the ego-self. Imagine peeling off and letting go of all that has been hindering your relationship with the divine—fears, anger, etc.]

❖

The second stage, illumination, *begins as you enter the center of the labyrinth, a place of prayer and meditation. In entering the center, the instruction is simple: enter with an open heart and mind. Receive what is there for you.* [The center of the labyrinth is the center of the mandala—the spiritual eye, the place of illumination. When you reach this stage, stay a while and meditate with focus in your spiritual eye, and as you go deeper, humbly ask for a symbol for your mandala.]

❖

The third stage is union *with the divine. People who have had an important experience in the center find that this third stage of the labyrinth provides a way to integrate the insight they have gained.*

❖

Others feel that the walk out of the labyrinth stokes the creative fires within, energizing the insight. The walk empowers, invites, and even pushes us to be more authentic and confident and risking with our gifts in the world.

❖

[See the revelatory symbol you receive in the center as a luminous divine gift and place it in your heart. In silence, empower the symbol by mentally chanting *Aum* three times. Then go out the same way you went in, meditating on what you have received. By completing the mandala drawing, you will honor and empower the revelation given you so that you can be more authentic in the world.]

❖

Merging the Ritual of the Labyrinth and Mandala

Mandalas are not restricted to drawings on paper. All over the world one can find temples constructed as three-dimensional mandalas. One can also find labyrinths, which are circular walkways created from sacred geometry. Walking in them allows you to become part of an integrating mandala reflecting universal wholeness. According to the Reverend Dr. Lauren Artress, Canon of Special Ministries at Grace Cathedral, labyrinths have been around for more than four thousand years and are found in every religious tradition. One can find them illustrated as line drawings in many books on mandalas. Yet it wasn't until I met Dr. Artress that I experienced the labyrinth as a fully alive and empowered mandalic symbol. She built at Grace Cathedral a replica of the Chartres Cathedral labyrinth, and she has used it to help thousands of people to reclaim mystical states of consciousness.

Lauren and I met at a conference on transpersonal psychology and became friends. We decided to collaborate on a spiritual retreat, combining the rituals of drawing the mandala and walking the labyrinth. The opportunity to integrate these two spiritual exercises in the environment of Grace Cathedral was an exciting spiritual prospect for me. We designed a silent retreat with people from all different ethnic and spiritual groups. The last meditation in this chapter (p. 135) is based on this collaboration. In the final stage of the retreat, participants shared in the silence to access the numinosity of their beings. The retreat honored all religions while seeing beyond their various outer forms to the central core that unites them.

There are labyrinths being developed throughout the United States and Europe. To locate a labyrinth near you, call or write to Quest/ Grace Cathedral, San Francisco, California. (See the resource section at the end of the book.) After you walk the labyrinth in meditation, draw a mandala to express and reflect the symbol released to you.

FIG. 6.6. THE LABYRINTH AT GRACE CATHEDRAL, SAN FRANCISCO, CALIFORNIA.

When we walk the labyrinth, the mysterious winding path becomes a metaphor for our own spiritual journey. It becomes a mirror reflecting the place where we stand in our lives . . . Walking the labyrinth clears the mind, gives insight into the spiritual journey, and urges action. It calms people and helps them to see their lives in the context of a faith path: a pilgrimage.

—The Reverend Dr. Lauren Artress, Canon of Special Ministries and
Director of the Labyrinth Project, Grace Cathedral

Summary: *One Light and Sound of All Truths*

The universe, our souls, all languages and symbols, and all truths of the various religions, arts, and sciences are manifested through the great *Aum* vibration or Word, the Divine Mother or creative aspect of God. Like ever-changing sonic mandalas, physical matter pulsates with aspects of this luminous sound of Creative Consciousness. We, as souls, as children of divinity, being a part of this sound, are endowed with latent spiritual gifts to mirror our part of this incandescent truth. However, misuse of physical energies and emphasis on our differences have mentally and emotionally separated us and have caused much sickness on Earth. If we could but grasp the truth of *Aum* we could foster, from a place of unconditional love and wisdom, the latent spiritual genius in everyone by honoring and respecting the various ways in which individuals and various cultures glorify God through sacred song, inspired scripture, and revelatory art and science. We are at a turning point in history, forced to make order out of our chaos. We must dust the darkness off our old ways of being and seeing by opening our hearts to higher states of intuition to see more clearly who we really are before we can be ultimately healed and reflect the clear Light of God.

The pilgrimage of the mystic soul is a sacred circular coming into light to creatively express and ultimately merge with the Divine Mother/Father, the One Light and Sound of us all. Through creative effort it is possible to awaken to this deepest truth of our nature and know our place in the universe. As we enter the next millennium, we are challenged to integrate our feminine and masculine selves, and to heal our sense of fragmentation. By letting go of our sense of separateness and aligning our wills with God's, we can become clear channels of revelation and solutions for personal and global healing. Many great people have gone before us to light our way—we need only open the spiritual eye to see and the spiritual ear to hear.

Notes

[1] Matthew Fox, ed., *Hildegard of Bingen's Book of Divine Works* (Santa Fe: Bear and Company, 1987), 6.

[2] Paramahansa Yogananda, *Autobiography of a Yogi* (Los Angeles: Self-Realization Fellowship, 1990) 568.

[3] Gabriele Uhlein, ed., *Meditations with Hildegard of Bingen* (Santa Fe: Bear and Company, 1982), 88-89.

[4] Fox, *Divine Works,* 26.

[5] Ibid., 67.

[6] Ibid., 128.

[7] Sri Ramakrishna, quoted by Yatri, *Unknown Man* (New York: Simon & Schuster Inc., 1988), 158.

[8] Thomas Cleary, trans., *The Secret of the Golden Flower* (San Francisco: HarperSan Francisco, 1991), 19.

[9] Sri Shankaranarayanan, *Sri Chakra* (Madras: Dipti Publications, 1979), 29.

Symbols of major world religions (from top, clockwise): Hinduism; Christianity; Judaism; Buddhism; Shintoism; Taoism; Native American religions; and Islam.

Afterword:

The Mandala in Jungian Psychotherapy

by Michael Flanagin, Ph.D.

Jung's discovery of the mandala provided the key to his entire system.

—Preface to C. G. Jung, *Mandala Symbolism*

C. G. Jung's Encounter With the Mandala

Fig. A (top right).

In the paintings of a woman undergoing Jungian psychotherapy, the initiatory contact with the unconscious self is portrayed as a bolt of lightning. The experience catalyzes a process of self-emergence reflected in the mandala-shaped rock that is broken free from the dark bedrock and represents the painter's potential wholeness.

At the beginning of the twentieth century, knowledge of the mandala in the West was confined largely to scholars of Hindu and Buddhist iconography. However, C. G. Jung, the pioneering explorer of the collective unconscious, first encountered the mandala not in a scholarly context, but in his efforts to relieve suffering—both his own and that of patients in psychotherapy. Jung had come to the realization that modern suffering was often related to the waning power of traditional religious symbolism to heal psychological fragmentation. Further, in the midst of a deep crisis in his own life, he discovered that sacred symbols—including the mandala—emerged spontaneously in both dreams and artwork to orchestrate wholeness and rebirth, independently of religion. To promote this process in his patients, Jung helped them to become conscious of the healing symbols generated naturally by their own unconscious psyches.

Jung's initial involvement with the mandala occurred during the First World War. The warfare in the outer world was mirrored by his own inner turmoil. Instinctively, he began sketching mandalas in his notebooks without knowing what they were, although he experienced their stabilizing emotional effects.

Once he understood that his mandala sketches symbolized his own inner process of self-renewal and self-realization, he stopped drawing them. However, it was some time before he would venture into print about his early mandala work. "For at least thirteen years I kept quiet about the results of these methods in order to avoid any suggestion. I wanted to assure myself," he wrote, "that these . . . mandalas . . . really are produced spontaneously and were not suggested to the patient by my own fantasy. I was then able to convince myself, through my own studies, that mandalas were drawn, painted, carved in stone, and built, at all times and in all parts of the world, long before my patients discovered them. I have also seen to my satisfaction that

mandalas are dreamt and drawn by patients who were being treated by psychotherapists whom I had not trained. In view of the importance and significance of the mandala symbol, special precautions seemed to be necessary, seeing that this motif is one of the best examples of the universal operation of an archetype."[1]

Jung provides a rich example of the role performed by drawing a mandala in his autobiography, *Memories, Dreams, Reflections*. At the

FIGURES A AND B COURTESY OF THE ESTATE OF C. G. JUNG, NIEDIECK LINDER AG, ZURICH, FROM C. G. JUNG, *MANDALA SYMBOLISM*.

FIG. B (preceding page).

Jung's patient painted the galvanizing energy from her unconscious psyche as a serpent that was transformed from the lightning bolt in the previous painting. The round boulder is now shown as a planet in space, much as a mandala forms as an artist meditates before the creative act.

time when he parted company with Sigmund Freud, Jung faced painful isolation, antagonism, and professional and psychological disorientation. It was during this time of turmoil that mandalas began to arise spontaneously to provide orientation and to integrate the unknown psychic material that was rising up from within his unconscious. He realized that it was apparently instinctual intuition that had caused him to draw the mandalas:

> I sketched every morning in a notebook a small circular drawing, a mandala, which seemed to correspond to my inner situation at the time. With the help of these drawings I could observe my psychic transformations from day to day . . . During those years, between 1918 and 1920, I began to understand that the goal of psychic development is the self.* There is no linear evolution; there is only a circumambulation of the self . . . This insight gave me stability, and gradually my inner peace returned. I knew that in finding the mandala as an expression of the self I had attained what was for me the ultimate.[2]

Jung's involvement with the mandala culminated in his insight that it represented the center, the midpoint that balances all dualities. This breakthrough marked his emergence from the darkness of disorientation to the light of a renewed perspective. In his autobiography, he narrates the powerful dream that illustrated this culmination:

> I found myself in a dirty, sooty city. It was night, and winter, and dark, and raining. I was in Liverpool. With a number of Swiss . . . I walked through the dark streets . . . we found a broad square dimly illumined by street lights, into which many streets converged. The various quarters of the city were arranged radially around the square. In the center was a round pool, and in the middle of it a small island. While everything round about was obscured by rain, fog, smoke, and dimly lit darkness, the little island blazed with sunlight. On it stood a single tree, a magnolia, in a shower of reddish blossoms. It was as though the tree stood in the sunlight and were at the same time the source of light. My companions commented on the abominable weather, and obviously did not see the tree. They spoke of another Swiss who was living in Liverpool, and expressed surprise that he should live here. I was carried away by the beauty of the flowering tree and the

*self/Self. Jung uses the term *self* to indicate a higher, or "super-ordinate" personality, that stands between ego-consciousness and the unconscious, expressing the gradual emergence of an integration of both as it is realized.

sunlit island, and thought, "I know very well why he has settled here."
Then I awoke.[3]

In this dream, the center of the mandala is bathed in beautiful
sunlight. This expresses the marriage of opposites, the transcendence of
duality, that occurs in the realization of the Self. Jung experienced this
transcendent wholeness as a radiating light. Visually, the light emanates
from the center to render the mandala visible, symbolizing psychologically how higher consciousness supplants and heals the self-division of
warring opposites. It is the function of the Self to promote higher
consciousness by integrating polarities, a process that represents itself
by the symbol of the mandala.

When Jung sought cultural parallels to illustrate the Self, such as
the life of Christ, the Buddha, or Krishna, he showed how these traditional religious figures were paradigms for an individual on a path of
Self-realization. This awareness of a higher inner Self—symbolized in
Jung's dream as light blossoming from a tree—led him beyond both
traditional religion and the need to sketch mandalas. Jung concluded
his narrative about the dream with the insight that he no longer needed
to sketch mandalas because he had completed the integrative process it
symbolized:

> *This dream brought with it a sense of finality. I saw that here the goal*
> *had been revealed. One could not go beyond the center. The center is the*
> *goal, and everything is directed toward that center. Through this dream*
> *I understood that the self is the principle and archetype of orientation*
> *and meaning. Therein lies its healing function. For me, this insight*
> *signified an approach to the center and therefore to the goal . . . After*
> *this dream I gave up drawing or painting mandalas. The dream depicted*
> *the climax of the whole process of development of consciousness.*[4]

In both dreams and religion, the relation of the center to the
mandala expresses the relation between the potential and the actual. In
the West, we generally imagine this process as going in one direction
(the actualization of potential), but in the East the path to liberation is
more likely to move from what is actual to a state of potential that
transcends form. The mandala embraces both directions, which is why
it is the consummate archetype of East and West alike. As the "alpha
and omega," the center is a union of opposites—a reflection of the true
higher Self. Jung writes:

> *When I began drawing the mandalas . . . I saw that everything, all the*

The shift from a traditional religious orientation to a direct relationship with one's inner imaginative resources is captured in a story Jung once told about a sage secluded in his cave. In a state of bewilderment comparable to Jung's own after his break from Freud, the sage began to sketch a mandala on the cave wall, again with instinctual intuition. Guided to Self-realization by creating the image, he quit the cave. Later, other seekers after truth (who expected it to be simply provided rather than wrested forth) stumble across the abandoned cave and see the mandala on the wall. They decide that this image represents the truth rather than the process that generated it. To understand the process that generates a mandala, each of its components must be explored.

paths I had been following, all the steps I had taken, were leading back to a single point—namely, to the mid-point. It became increasingly plain to me that the mandala is the center. It is the exponent of all paths. It is the path to the center, to individuation.[5]

Although the religious traditions of the East depict the realization of the higher Self in elaborate metaphysical imagery, Jungian psychology reveals that this process is in fact an expression of a natural development of the psyche. By showing that dreams involve the marriage of opposites and their transcendence by a superior, integrated personality (represented abstractly by a mandala), Jung actively demonstrated the natural impulse of the psyche toward integration.

Alchemy is a Western symbolic path for this process of integration which Jung investigated to explore a cultural parallel to dream symbolism, especially mandala symbolism. Just as the Hindu divinities of male and female cosmic energy, Shiva and Shakti, are conjoined in a round mandala, so King and Queen as alchemical sulphur and silver are mixed in the alchemist's round glass vessel. Alchemy had a great significance for Jung, in that it reflected a worldview unifying psyche and matter, a transformation through the integration of opposites that served as an analogy to the goals of psychotherapy.

Synchronicity: *Unity of Matter and Psyche*

Nobel physicist Wolfgang Pauli and Jung co-authored the groundbreaking book *Interpretation of Nature and the Psyche*, which contains Jung's original statements about synchronicity. That a nuclear physicist, with a focus on matter and physical reality, and a depth psychologist, with a focus on the psyche and symbolism, should collaborate on a creative interpretation of reality is the very demonstration of the unifying trend emerging in modern thought. Jung named the principle operating within reality "synchronicity" to express the underlying unity of matter and psyche. This was one of the first intimations in our century of a nondual perspective arising not in religion but in science. Synchronicity is seen as a reflection not of cause and effect but as of meaningful coincidences. In the state of consciousness natural to the field within the mandala—that of Self-realization, or nonduality—such opposites as inner and outer, or subjective and objective, male or female, matter and spirit, are all grasped as connected, married, ultimately unified. This vision, though traditional and natural within the Tibetan Buddhist canon, was revolutionary within a Western, dualistic perspective.

Both religious canon and Jung himself acknowledged that the perceptions of higher unity and heightened significance natural to the field within the mandala—that is the state of consciousness which the mandala develops in concert with the meditator—can be overwhelming, suggesting that transformation be initiated in an environment of loving support. This is why the mandala is protected by a ring of flames, and why subtle and guarded initiations are woven into the Tibetan canon. It is no accident that Jung discovered the mandala in the context of psychiatry. The mandala often is constellated naturally to heal and protect such profound transformative experiences.

The Tension of Opposites

Jung made a great deal of the tension of opposites and perceived the mandala as their reconciliation. Ego-consciousness typically identifies with one polarity or the other (e.g., masculine versus feminine, intellect versus feeling, materialism versus spirituality), and suppresses its opposite into the unconscious. When this pattern becomes extreme, as in people who would seek out Jungian analysis, the unconscious, often through a painful symptom, initiates a process that tends toward the restoration of balance—a state in which both opposing poles may be held in conscious, creative harmony by a center that unifies them. It is this resolution that a mandala symbolizes, and this explains its power to heal and transform psychologically.

FIG. C (top left).

In this painting the woman depicted the serpent penetrating into the core of the mandala image. Within the center of the mandala, the serpent plants a seed, using a biological metaphor to symbolize a spiritual union of the masculine and feminine that prefigures the artist's emerging wholeness.

FIG. D (bottom left).

As the woman completed her psychotherapy with Jung in Switzerland, she returned to America. In this painting of a mandala she shows how her inner realization allows for a creative relationship with the outer world, shown as the night skyline of Fifth Avenue in New York City.

A pair of opposites in this book that constitutes its motif is that between light and darkness—or in Jungian interpretation, between that which is conscious and that which is unconscious. Importantly, in Jung's psychology, light follows the realization of darkness (or the making of the unconscious conscious). This suggests a greater light than the relative consciousness of the ego, which is generally identified with a polarity. Such a transcendent light is described in the prologue to the Gospel of John as "a light which the darkness does not overtake." It reflects the consciousness inherent in the Self—the center of the mandala—rather than the ego.

"Whereas ritual mandalas," Jung writes, "always display a definite style and a limited number of typical motifs as their content, individual mandalas make use of a well-nigh unlimited wealth of motifs and symbolic allusions, from which it can easily be seen that they are endeavoring to express either the totality of the individual in his inner or outer experience of the world, or its essential point of reference. Their object is the *self* in contradistinction to the *ego*, which is only the point of reference for consciousness, whereas the self comprises the totality of the psyche altogether, i.e., conscious *and* unconscious. It is therefore not unusual for individual mandalas to display a division into a light and a dark half, together with their typical symbols."[6]

From this perspective, the dark half may be perceived as the source of light, or of a greater light that follows the sacrifice of the relative limits of ego-consciousness as a lesser light. This is a painful sacrifice, one that requires trust, surrender, and the realization that a higher identity follows the death of a lower identity. Some might seek such an ordeal intentionally, but usually life itself thrusts it upon an individual. When this happens, the darkness may appear as a protracted period of isolation, depression, or, among artists, a lull in creative output. The mandala may arise in dreams, perhaps as a light that dawns from above a dark ocean, or as a compelling image, as in appealing interlocking circles or wheels, that the artist sketches automatically because of it agreeable feeling-tone. "Even the mere attempt in this direction," Jung explains, "usually has a healing effect, but only when it is done sponta-neously. Nothing can be expected from an artificial repetition or a deliberate imitation of such images."[7]

The Stirring of the Unlived Life: *A Case Illustration*

In *Study in the Process of Individuation,* Jung recounts the case of a woman who began an encounter with the unconscious psyche in the second half of her life.[8] She turned away from her role as "daughter of her father" when her natural maternal aspect, never actualized, began stirring and pressing for realization. Traveling to Denmark, prompted by an instinct that led her to the birthplace of her mother, this woman began painting images of her psychological state, and these paintings eventually led her to contact Jung in Switzerland.

In the first painting, the artist depicted herself as if the lower half of her body (i.e., the unconscious) were embedded in rocks alongside the Danish seacoast. Next, she painted a dream in which a sorcerer on the beach freed her with an intense stroke of energy. In her painting of this event, a lightning bolt loosened a round boulder from the rocky beach. The round boulder is the first intimation of the mandala, and it has within it (Fig. A) a swirling warm-color brush stroke that resembles the yoke of an egg. Her separation from the bedrock—the unreflecting and inert mass-mindedness that our entire psychic life has as its original source—indicates that the long path to conscious self-realization has begun.

In the next painting (Fig. B), the lightning bolt has been transformed into a hovering gold snake and the round boulder appears to be a planet floating in the heavens. This poised moment shifts in the next painting (Fig. C) to one of seeming sexual or biological conception—but the meaning is more precisely psychological. The snake—the active or dynamic aspect of the life of the unconscious psyche—is black and thrusts head-first into the core of the mandala image. In the core's interior is a receptacle into which the serpent has implanted a gold seed, and the suggestion of a feminine vessel or womb is combined with the symmetry of a plant pod.

Outside the outer border is mere empty space painted in a dull brown. This space represents the world outside the analytic chamber (physically) and outside the analytic process (psychologically). Within is an intermediate gold zone in which the serpent moves, and this is the analyst's zone, a field that in technical therapeutic jargon is aptly named "the container." The mandala is a container for the engagement of opposites and forces that must not be spilled into the outer world if their transformative effect is to unfold. On the other hand, these elements cannot remain merely in embryo in the very core—so a dialogue is set up between the masculine and feminine principles of the psyche, using the perennial metaphor of conception and gestation.

In the following paintings, the serpent withdraws, and the mandala unfolds like a zygote, its original central point having multiplied into a fourfold or four-petaled design. This unfolding continues as, under the guidance of her analyst, the woman begins to realize a new dimension of her personality. But in the middle of this series of about two dozen paintings, a mandala appears that floats against the background of New

York City (Fig. D). In outer reality, she returned to America, and this painting depicts the consolidation of her inner life against the backdrop of the Manhattan skyline. There, in a highly creative development, she established an analytic training center to perpetuate the experience she herself had experienced in Europe. One of the final paintings (Fig. E) gives a graphic account of this: a mandala of six round images, each of which is shown with a smaller disk rising over a horizon. In one of the round images a green snake rises over a sun shown on the horizon—perhaps at sea—and breaks out of the outer periphery of the mandala.

If this account interprets the visual narrative of this woman's paintings correctly, she documents in Fig. E the very process that she first experienced in Fig. A. The correspondence to this in her outer life is the beginning of her work as a training analyst, whereby she guided the process she experienced herself earlier, but now within her professional "progeny." In this way, but on a psychological plane rather than on a biological one, she lived out her maternal dimension. A Freudian psychoanalyst would consider her instinctuality to be merely sublimated, as suggested by the blatantly sexual forms of her paintings, but in fact the paintings document her creative journey to self-fulfillment and wholeness, with the aspirations of the psyche transcending the biological ones.

The balance and wholeness that this woman achieved is expressed in the final painting she created at the end of her life (see Fig. F). Here a radiant flower emerges from the center of a dark field, resting on top of the initiatory serpents and balanced from above by a single star of self-realized consciousness. The natural wholeness seems to show that the feminine has been integrated into her psyche. And in its role as a container, this mandala—like all mandalas—can be seen as an expression of the feminine form.

Jung's discovery that the mandala arises spontaneously out of the depths of the psyche reveals that the mandala may be seen as belonging to each of us within, emerging in the encounter between opposing forces, however painful this may be. Such an encounter promotes consciousness, and higher consciousness is demanded if mutual understanding and a solution to world problems are to be achieved. In his connection of an inner mandala to the crisis of the outer world, one of Jung's successors, Marie-Louise von Franz, identifies a time of healing that has long awaited the marriage of opposites—inner and outer, masculine and feminine—opposites that have been split apart in our culture for too many centuries.

The emergence of the mandala in the spiritual and artistic imagination of various pioneering figures of our century anticipates a new consciousness that can contain these opposites simultaneously. Von Franz sees this fusion as a balancing response to the one-sided masculine principle that has prevailed for at least the last 2,000 years, and probably dating back several millennia: "The masculine drive toward activity and Faustian aggressiveness—caught in the maternal womb of the mandala—can only there be transformed into a new creative form in which the destructive initiative of our existence can be integrated."[9]

FIG. E (top left).

Painted late in the series, this image illustrates how the process initiated by the serpent repeats itself in the form of a snake in an egg released from the woman's mandala. The artist, who began to train students in Jungian psychotherapy, now mothered a similar process of spiritual growth in other people.

FIG. F (bottom left).

In her final painting before her death, the artist portrayed the peaceful harmony and illumined wholeness that resulted from her encounter with Jungian psychotherapy. Self-realization is represented as a luminous flower, supported by the serpents that initiated the creation of the mandala.

FIGURES E AND F COURTESY OF THE ESTATE OF C. G. JUNG, NIEDIECK LINDER AG, ZURICH, FROM C. G. JUNG, MANDALA SYMBOLISM.

Notes

[1] Jung, C. G., *Archetypes and the Collective Unconscious* (Princeton: Princeton University Press, 1969), 352-53.

[2] Jung, C. G., *Memories, Dreams, and Reflections* (New York: Pantheon Books, 1961), 195f.

[3] Ibid., 197-98.

[4] Ibid., 198-99.

[5] Ibid., 196.

[6] Jung, C. G., *Archetypes and the Collective Unconscious*, 389.

[7] Ibid., 390.

[8] Jung, C. G. "A Study in the Process of Individuation," in *Archetypes and the Collective Unconscious.* Vol. 9i of the *Collected Works* (Princeton: Princeton University Press, 1969).

[9] von Franz, Marie-Louise, *C. G. Jung: His Myth in Our Time* (New York: C. G. Jung Foundation for Analytical Psychology/Putnam, 1975), 147.

APPENDIX 1

A Guide to Using the CD with this Book

GETTING STARTED

Before you begin have ready the following art supplies:

Sanford Prismacolor Pencils

Sanford Prismacolor drawing pencils will give good results for creating luminous white light and rainbow effects on black paper. You can find them in most office or art supply stores and can also purchase them through Judith Cornell's website, www.mandala-universe.com/bookstore6. Especially recommended are the following colors (2 white pencils plus one each of 6 colored pencils):

> White #PC938
> Spring Green #PC913
> Magenta #PC930
> Aquamarine #PC905
> Orange #PC918
> Violet #PC932
> Canary Yellow #PC916

Paper

Unless otherwise specified, you may use any black heavyweight construction paper. When larger paper is requested and if you want a better quality, use 19 x 25 inch black charcoal paper or a Strathmore 500 Series spiral-bound black charcoal paper pad.

1. Exercise: Creating a Scale of Light

Procedure:

- Before you begin, view the illustrations on pages 20–21.
- Sharpen two white Prismacolor pencils.
- Prepare a square sheet of black paper as illustrated in figure 1.4 on page 21.
- Have ready the two sharpened pencils and the small square from the sheet of black paper.
- Listen to CD, track 1 and follow the instructions to create your own vibrant sensation of light.

2. Meditation: Remembering Who You Are

Procedure:

- Before you begin, bookmark pages 22–25 for quick reference.
- Sharpen two white Prismacolor pencils.
- Prepare a second square of black paper as illustrated in figure 1.4 on page 21.
- Listen to CD, track 2 with your eyes closed. Then open your eyes and complete the exercise, "Expanding the Light Within," on page 25.

3. Meditation: Blessing the Materials, and

4. Exercise: Drawing the Outline of Your Hands

Procedure:

- Before you begin, bookmark pages 42–43 and study the illustrations for the exercise.
- Sharpen two white Prismacolor drawing pencils.
- Use a template to draw a circle approximately 17 to 18 inches in diameter on a large 19 x 24 inch sheet of black charcoal paper.
- Place the two sharpened pencils and the sheet of black paper in your lap.
- Follow the instructions in CD, tracks 3 and 4 in succession.

5. Meditation: Bringing Prana through the Hands

Procedure:

- Before you begin, bookmark pages 46–49 and study the examples of luminous hand drawings.
- Have ready the circle drawing of the outline of your hands on black paper and two sharpened white pencils.
- Listen to CD, track 5 with your eyes closed.
- Follow the instructions to access and illustrate the healing energies within you.

6. Meditation: Accessing a Healing Symbol

Procedure:

- Before you begin, bookmark pages 66–67.
- Have ready black paper, two sharpened white Prismacolor pencils, a circle template, and a journal in which to write your healing intention.
- Place before you a lighted candle or incense and an image of a spiritual master such as Buddha or Christ.
- Listen to CD, track 6, following the instructions to illuminate the symbol you receive in meditation (see illustrations on page 67).

7. Exercise: Creating a Luminous Mandala, and

8. Meditation: Accessing Healing Colors

Procedure:

- Before you begin, bookmark pages 84–89.
- Have ready six rainbow-colored sharpened pencils and a sheet of black paper.
- Listen to CD, track 7.
- Then pause track 8 and complete the three color exercises on pages 84–89 on the sheet of black paper.
- Have ready the drawing of your black-and-white healing symbol from exercise 6.
- Listen to the Healing Colors meditation, track 8.
- Bring those colors into your luminous black and white drawing.

9. Meditation: Journeys into the Divine Realities of Nature, and

10. Exercise: Symbolic Drawing of Birds and Animals

Procedure:

- Before you begin, bookmark and read pages 101–110.

- Sharpen two white and six rainbow-colored pencils.
- Have ready a circle template and a large sheet of black paper.
- Follow the instructions on CD, tracks 9 and 10 in succession.

PRAISE FOR JUDITH CORNELL

I have attended many, many presentations. None can compare with Judith's work in value or meaning for the participants. I truly experienced a shift in consciousness. My life will not be the same—is not the same.

—Pat Sommers, Board of Directors, Unity Church, Chesterland, Ohio

I found Judith's mandala process for cancer patients full of inspiration, creativity, and empowerment for all participants. It gave us the opportunity to delve deep inside ourselves to find amazing strength, joy, and inner guidance to assist us in true healing. There is a great need to bring the sacred back into the medical community, and Judith's mandala process offers that opportunity.

—Patty Cashman, R.N., hospice nurse, chaplain, and cancer support group facilitator, Mercy Medical Center, Mount Shasta, California

APPENDIX 2

Suggested Resources

ADDITIONAL HEALING SUPPORT BY JUDITH CORNELL

Facilitation Training

Dr. Cornell bases this training for professionals on her new book, *Mandala Healing: Using Spiritual Symbols for Spiritual and Emotional Healing*. It is especially appropriate for broadminded professionals in various fields of service who are open to all faith traditions, who are continuing to deepen their own spiritual practice, and who are willing to let go of ego and serve selflessly. The training teaches ways to:

• Lead heart-based support groups through practice break-out sessions

• Help those in life-challenging situations obtain spiritual and emotional support

• Help people view such situations as rites of passage and opportunities for growth

• Facilitate specific healing and transformation exercises

The training offers Continuing Education Credit for nurses, MFT/MFCC's, and LCSW's.

For more information and a current list of facilitation trainings and retreats, visit Dr. Cornell's website, www.mandala-universe.com/events, or call 800-833-4668.

Life Coaching and Individual Healing Sessions for Cancer Patients

As an ongoing service, Dr. Cornell now offers individual sessions for those challenged by cancer. Learn ways to reduce suffering and handle stress-filled life situations. Learn how you can participate in your healing by working with your creative energies to achieve the greatest possible wellness in body, mind, and spirit. For more information, visit Dr. Cornell's webpage, www.mandala-universe.com/events2.html, or call 800-833-4668.

ORGANIZATIONS AND INFORMATION

Holos University

The Holos University Graduate Seminary (HUGS) is the original doctoral program for those interested in the principles of Complementary and Alternative Medicine, Energy Medicine, and Spiritual Healing and Spiritual Direction (see www.hugs-edu.org). Presently Dr. Cornell is assistant professor in the department of Transpersonal Psychology at Holos. Those interested in a degree in Transpersonal Psychology can receive credit for taking any of the Mandala courses listed on Dr. Cornell's events page (www.mandala-universe.com/events.html). Holos students may select any of Dr. Cornell's listed workshops to fulfill the residential component of the 885: Mandala course. This 3-credit-hour course is a requirement for the Holos degree in Transpersonal Psychology.

The International Society for the Study of Subtle Energies and Energy Medicine (ISSSEEM)

This society is an international nonprofit interdisciplinary organization dedicated to exploring and applying subtle energies as they relate to the experience of consciousness, healing, and human potential. For more information, see www.issseem.org.

C. Norman Shealy, M.D., Ph.D.

Dr. Shealy's website provides a newsletter and information on self-health systems, vitamins and nutritional supplements, and a wealth of carefully considered research (see http://www.normshealy.net).

BIBLIOGRAPHY

BOOKS

Bakhtiar, Laleh. *Sufi: Expressions of the Mystic Quest.* New York: Thames and Hudson, 1976.

Becker, Robert 0. *Cross Currents: The Perils of Electropollution, The Promise of Electromedicine.* Los Angeles: Tarcher, 1989.

————. *The Body Electric: Electromagnetism and the Foundation of Life.* New York: Morrow, 1985.

Benson, Herbert, M.D. *Your Maximum Mind.* New York: Times Books, Random House, 1987.

Birnbaum, Raoul. *The Healing Buddha.* Boston: Shambhala, 1979.

Blavatsky, H. P. *The Secret Doctrine: The Synthesis of Science, Religion, and Philosophy.* Pasadena: Theosophical University Press, 1977.

Bohm, David. *Wholeness and the Implicate Order.* London: Routlege, Chatman, and Paul, 1980.

Bohm, David, and F. David Peat. *Science, Order, Creativity.* New York: Bantam Books, 1987.

Brennan, Barbara. *Hands of Light: A Guide to Healing through the Human Energy Field.* New York: Bantam, 1988.

Brooks, Douglas Renfrew. *The Secret of the Three Cities: An Introduction to Hindu Sakta Tantrism.* Chicago: University of Chicago Press, 1990.

Campbell, Joseph. *Historical Atlas of World Mythology.* New York: Harper & Row, 1988.

Chögyam, Ngakpa. *Rainbow of Liberated Energy.* Dorset, England: Element Books, 1986.

Cleary, Thomas, trans. *The Secret of the Golden Flower.* San Francisco: HarperSanFrancisco, 1991.

Clifford, Terry. *Tibetan Buddhist Medicine and Psychiatry: The Diamond Healing.* York Beach, ME: Samuel Weiser, 1984.

Dacher, Elliott S., M.D. *PNI: The New Mind/ Body Healing Program.* New York: Paragon, 1992.

Donden, Dr. Yeshi. *Health through Balance: An Introduction to Tibetan Medicine.* Ithaca, New York: Snow Lion Publications, 1986.

Einstein, Albert. *Essays in Science.* New York: The Philosophical Library Inc., 1934.

Eliade, Mircea. *The Two and the One.* New York: Harper & Row, 1965.

Evans-Wentz, W. Y, ed. *Tibetan Yoga and Secret Doctrines.* London: Oxford University Press, 1958.

Gold, Peter. *Navaho and Tibetan Sacred Wisdom: The Circle of Spirit.* Rochester, VT: Inner Traditions, 1994.

Govinda, Lama Anagarika. *Creative Meditation and Multi-Dimensional Consciousness.* Wheaton, IL: Theosophical Publishing House, Quest Books, 1976.

————. *The Way of the White Clouds: A Buddhist Pilgrim in Tibet.* Boulder: Shambhala, 1970.

Hawking, Stephen. *A Brief History of Time.* New York: Bantam Books, 1990.

Hildegard of Bingen's Book of Divine Works. Edited by Matthew Fox. Santa Fe: Bear and Company, 1987.

Huyler, Stephen P. *Painted Prayers: Women's Art in Village India.* New York: Rizzoli, 1994.

Illuminations of Hildegard of Bingen. Edited by Matthew Fox. Santa Fe: Bear and Company, 1985.

Jung, C. G. *Man and His Symbols.* Garden City, NY: Doubleday & Company, Inc., 1964.

————. *Mandala Symbolism.* Princeton: Princeton University Press, 1973.

————. *Memories, Dreams, Reflections.* New York: Pantheon Books, 1961.

————. *On the Nature of the Psyche.* Princeton: Princeton University Press, 1973.

————. *Psychology and Alchemy.* Vol. 12 of the *Collected Works.* New York: Pantheon Books, 1973.

————. "A Study in the Process of Individuation." *Archetypes and the Collective Unconscious.* Vol. 9i of *The Collected Works.* Princeton: Princeton University Press, 1969.

Jung, C. G., with Wolfgang Pauli. *The Interpretation of Nature and Psyche.* New York: Pantheon Books, 1955.

Khanna, Madhu. *Yantra: The Tantric Symbol of Cosmic Unity.* London: Thames and Hudson Ltd., 1979.

Krishna, Gopi. *The Dawn of a New Science.* New Delhi: Kundalini Research and Publication Trust, 1978.

Lauf, Detlef. *Tibetan Sacred Art— The Heritage of Tantra.* Berkeley and London: Shambhala, 1976.

Leidy, Denise Patry and Robert A. F. Thurman. *Mandala: The Architecture of Enlightenment.* Boston: Shambhala, 1997.

Lightman, Alan. *Ancient Light: Our Changing View of the Universe.* Cambridge: Harvard University Press, 1991.

Locke, Steven M.D., and Douglas Colligan. *The Healer Within: The New Medicine of Mind and Body.* New York: E. P. Dutton, 1990.

Lowenstein, Jerold M. "Molecular Approaches to the Indentification of Species." *American Scientist* 73 (Nov.–Dec. 1985).

McGaa, Ed, Eagle Man. *Mother Earth Spirituality, Native American Paths to Healing Ourselves and Our World.* San Francisco: HarperSanFrancisco, 1990.

Meditations with Hildegard of Bingen. Edited by Gabriele Uhlein. Santa Fe: Bear and Company, 1982.

Meera, Mother. *Answers.* London: Rider, Random Century Group, 1991.

Mookerjee, Ajit. *Kundalini, The Arousal of the Inner Energy.* Rochester, VT: Destiny Books, 1989.

————. *Tantric Art.* New Delhi: Ravi Kumar Publisher, 1983.

————. *The Tantric Way: Art, Science, Ritual.* London: Thames and Hudson Ltd., 1977.

Peat, F. David. "Light and Life." *The Philosopher's Stone: Chaos, Synchronicity, and the Hidden Order of the World.* New York: Bantam Books, 1991.

Plato. *The Republic: Book X.* Roslyn, NY: Walter J. Black, Inc., Classics Club edition, 1942.

Rao, S. K. Ramachandra. *Yantras.* Delhi, India: Sri Satguru Publications, 1988.

Sandner, Donald. *Navaho Symbols of Healing.* New York: Harcourt Brace Jovanovich, Inc., 1979.

Sperry, Roger. *Science and Moral Priority: Merging Mind, Brain, and Human Values.* New York: Columbia University Press, 1983.

Sri Shankaranarayanan. *Sri Chakra.* Madras, India: Dipti Publications, Sri Aurobindo Ashram, 1979.

Tapasyananda, Swami. *Sundarya-Lahari of Sri Sankaracarya.* Madras, India: Sri Ramakrishna Math, 1987.

Tucci, Giuseppe. *The Theory and Practice of the Mandala.* New York: Samuel Weiser, 1973.

Wilhelm, Richard, trans. *The Secret of the Golden Flower, with a Foreword and Commentary by C. G. Jung.* New York: Harcourt Brace Jovanovich, 1962.

Yeshe, Lama, *Introduction to Tantra: A Vision of Totality.* Boston: Wisdom Publications, 1987.

Yogananda, Paramahansa. *Autobiography of a Yogi.* Los Angeles: Self-Realization Fellowship, 1990.

———. *Man's Eternal Quest and Other Talks.* Los Angeles: Self-Realization Fellowship, 1988.

———. *Scientific Healing Affirmations.* Los Angeles: Self-Realization Fellowship, 1990.

———. *Where There Is Light.* Los Angeles: Self-Realization Fellowship, 1988.

Zimmer, Heinrich. *Artistic Form and Yoga in the Sacred Images of India.* Princeton: Princeton University Press, 1984.

WEBSITES

Hinduism

For information on Stephen Huyler's *Meeting God: Elements of Hindu Devotion,* see *www.huntingtonarchive. osu.edu/exhib/meetgod/hp.htm*

Tibetan Buddhism

For information on John C. Huntington's *The Circles of Bliss: Buddhist Meditational Art,* see *www.huntingtonarchive. osu.exhib/circleofbliss*

Sufism

See *www.sufiorder.org/*

Taoism

See *www.religion-cults.com/Eastern/ Taoism/taoism.htm*

Christianity

Hildegard of Bingen (1098–1179) was a remarkable Benedictine nun born in Germany. In an age when few women wrote, she was called the "Sybil of the Rhine" and produced major visionary works and illuminated mandalas. While few women were accorded respect, she was consulted by bishops, popes, and kings. See *www.fordham.edu/halsall/med/ hildegarde.html*

Native American Spirituality

For a PDF of John G. Neihardt's *Black Elk Speaks,* see *www.blackelkspeaks.unl.edu/ blackelk.pdf*

For information on the Medicine Wheel, see *www.geocities.com/ RainForest/Canopy/1835/*

Depth Psychology

For the mandalas of C. G. Jung (1875–1961), Swiss psychiatrist and founder of analytical psychology, see *www.netreach. net/~nhojem/jung.htm*

Quest Books
encourages open-minded inquiry into
world religions, philosophy, science, and the arts
in order to understand the wisdom of the ages,
respect the unity of all life, and help people explore
individual spiritual self-transformation.

Its publications are generously supported by
The Kern Foundation,
a trust committed to Theosophical education.

Quest Books is the imprint of
the Theosophical Publishing House,
a division of the Theosophical Society in America.
For information about programs, literature,
on-line study, membership benefits, and international centers,
see www.theosophical.org
or call 800-669-1571 or (outside the U.S.) 630-668-1571.

Related Quest Titles

Drawing from the Heart, Barbara Ganim

Drawing the Light from Within, Judith Cornell

God Is at Eye Level: Photography as a Healing Art, Jan Phillips

Mandala, Luminous Symbols for Healing (DVD), Judith Cornell

Marry Your Muse, Jan Phillips

Visual Journaling, Barbara Ganim and Susan Fox

To order books or a complete Quest catalog,
call 800-669-9425 or (outside the U.S.) 630-665-0130.